AN APPLE A

DAYS

ALEXANDER TULLOCH

SUTTON PUBLISHING

First published in 2006 by
Sutton Publishing Limited · Phoenix Mill
Thrupp · Stroud · Gloucestershire · GL5 2BU

British Library Cataloguing in Publication Data
A catalogue record for this book is available from the British Library.

ISBN 0-7509-4318-1

Typeset in 10.5/13pt Galliard.
Typesetting and origination by
Sutton Publishing Limited.
Printed and bound in England by
J.H. Haynes & Co. Ltd, Sparkford.

Contents

Preface

This is not an autobiography. Certainly, the book contains a good deal of autobiographical information but at the same time much has been omitted. The reason for this is quite simple: I did not wish to risk boring the reader with superfluous material which would have contributed little or nothing to the general purpose and ethos of the book. When I set out to describe life in Liverpool after the end of the war my main aim was to give present and future generations an idea of what it was like to live in an age that has long passed into history. I wanted to evoke a time when life was less complicated, when pleasures were simple and a relative lack of money did not seem to stand in the way of our enjoyment of life. This was a time when there was no central heating and we huddled round a coal fire in an attempt to stay warm in winter but, when the summer sun made the inside of our tiny houses almost unbearable, we still had to have a coal fire to heat the water! This was a time when, for entertainment, we played Ludo and snakes and ladders in the evening or sat gathered round the radio. In the 1950s we supported church socials on Saturday nights, even if we never went to church on Sunday mornings; cars, fridges and even televisions were a rarity, and computers, iPods and mobile phones were beyond our wildest imaginings. But we could derive as much enjoyment spending five bob on a night out as today's younger generation does after spending the better part of a hundred pounds. It all seems very different from today's world.

The fifties were a time when a sense of loss could exist side by side with a sense of hope. For many who were middle-aged or in their declining years the nightmare memory of the Second World War and what it had taken from them was still fresh; for the younger generation it was already ancient history. The older generation was still readjusting, but the younger was looking forward, bursting with energy and a creative drive that was to reshape the new world just over the horizon. They were exciting times, and before the decade was out the old world would be left far behind, surviving only in the minds of writers, historians and other chroniclers of the human condition who believed that they should never be forgotten.

In writing this book I have occasionally experienced amnesia when memories of over fifty years ago became slightly blurred. On such occasions my sister Margaret has been an invaluable source of information and has frequently been able to remind me of people, places and events which had faded in my memory or I had quite simply forgotten. Without her gentle prodding such details could have slumbered in the deepest recesses of my increasingly forgetful mind, probably for ever. My thanks to her for her help.

PALACE CINEMA   WARBRECK SEC. MOD. SCHOOL   BLACK BULL PUB   CEDAR ROAD METHODIST CHURCH   WALTON VALE CINEMA

A bird's eye view of the part of Aintree where the author grew up. *(Liverpool Record Office)*

On those very few occasions when memory failed us both I have resorted to a little artistic reconstruction to paper over the gaps in the narrative. I hope none of this literary sticking plaster will detract from the overall effect of these recollections and happy memories or interfere with the reader's appreciation of my efforts to recall times past.

In addition to my sister there are other people to whom I would like to express my gratitude for their contribution to this book. I have to thank the staff of the Liverpool Record Office for the cheery Scouse way in which they helped me on a recent visit to the William Brown Library when I needed to find the old photographs of Liverpool which feature here. Thanks also to Mr David Gee of the Craig-Ard in Llandudno for sending me an up-to-date photograph of his hotel, and to Keith Wilson and Sian Stephens of the We Three Loggerheads for providing a picture of their hostelry.

Most of the names mentioned in *Aintree Days* are real. In a few cases, however, I thought it better to substitute fictitious names where there was a danger of my causing embarrassment or annoyance, or both.

1

The Warrior Returns

'Does nobody get a cuppa tea in this house any more? Anyone would think the bloody war was still on!' I didn't recognise the voice from downstairs, but could hear my mother laughing and joking with someone to the accompanying jingle of cups and saucers and the thumping and banging of the plumbing as she put the kettle on. The next thing I heard was my father coughing and asking if anyone had seen his fags.

It was still dark as I swung out of bed and suddenly felt the freezing cold lino as it seemed to spring off the floor and make contact with my feet. The noises from downstairs were now getting louder and louder as other members of the household, namely my grandparents, also made their way downstairs to greet the stranger. I joined them as fast as my little legs would carry me, but as I was only three or four years old at the time, the stairs were still a major obstacle and I had to control my enthusiasm to reach the bottom or suffer a nasty bump on the head if I fell downstairs and banged it on the monks' bench at the bottom.

When I reached the kitchen where they were all standing I saw this figure in a blue uniform wearing a funny hat which looked to me like one of the paper bags which had the chips in when Mum brought fish 'n' chips from the chippie. It was years later that I understood that the uniform was that of a flight sergeant in the RAF and the man standing in front of me was my uncle Alex, on leave for only the first or second time since the end of the Second World War.

'Hello', he said as I walked through the door, 'Who's this then . . . Wee Al?' Without waiting for a reply he picked me up and started tickling me, all the time breathing his tobacco smoke into my

Alexander Guthrie, the author's uncle. He was a Flight Sergeant in the RAF when this photo was taken during the Second World War. (*Author's collection*)

Margaret Tulloch, the author's mother, 1941. *(Author's collection)*

face. 'Here,' he said, taking a bar of something out of his pocket, 'would you like some chocolate?'

After that I don't remember anything else about that morning. I can't even remember if I ever ate the chocolate or what it tasted like. All I know was that the man who offered it to me was to keep popping up throughout my childhood, because although the war was over he stayed on in the forces and I would probably have forgotten him altogether had it not been for the airmail letters he sent home from places like Cyprus, Hong Kong and somewhere in Africa with a name that sounded very strange to me and which I never could pronounce.

This was Liverpool in the mid to late forties. Battered, bloody but unbowed after all the bombing, with its defiant Liver Birds still towering over the pierhead. And Aintree, despite the fact that my mother always said it was one of the better parts of the city, was a grim place to be. The bomb damage was horrendous. The tiny houses were probably long overdue for demolition before Hitler decided to come to the aid of the City Council and create vast open spaces where the Victorians had erected houses for the workers. But things were not so bad there as they were a few miles down the road towards the centre of Liverpool. That part of the city was like a wasteland. When we sat upstairs on the tram as it clanked along Rice Lane, Walton Road and then on to what seemed to me like the end of the earth, all that we could see through the grimy windows was mile after mile of bombed-out buildings or the distorted, twisted skeletons of offices and shops and what had once been family homes. As my grandfather used to say in his inimitably sardonic manner, 'At least Jerry cleared the slums a damn sight faster than the Council did.'

I've been a cigarette smoker since the day I was born. There were six of us in the family (me, my sister, Mum and Dad and the grandparents), and the four adults smoked from the moment they opened their eyes in the morning until they got into bed at night. So, as we now know, I was smoking all the time too. Fag after fag we smoked, all day, coughing, coughing, coughing, and there was smoke from the ceiling down to my knees so I can honestly say I never saw daylight through the sitting-room window. Even on bright sunny days all I saw was the roof on the house opposite through a kind of dirty yellow haze that passed for the atmosphere in our house. In those days nobody knew smoking was harmful and the term passive smoking was thirty years into the future: my mother even believed it was good for you as it killed the germs and kept the fleas away. It never occurred to her that the absence of fleas in the house might have been because (to her credit) she kept the house spotless. No. Smoke was the answer. Vermin hated it so she puffed away and encouraged everyone else to do so as well. In this way the germs and fleas and mice

Bob Tulloch, the author's father, during a break in a cricket match in the 1930s. (*Author's collection*)

and every other nasty creature would leave us alone and take up residence in a non-smoker's home. She also had the strange idea that it was good for the teeth, as a good coating of tar protected them from whatever it was that caused tooth decay. 'So why', I used to think to myself, 'has everybody in this family got false teeth?'

Then there was the watch. Kensitas, the cigarettes my mother smoked, introduced a coupon scheme allowing smokers to save up the vouchers in each packet in exchange for a free gift. I can't remember the figure, but for God knows how many vouchers you could get a free wrist-watch. One year, as my dad's birthday was looming on the horizon, she decided his present would be a Kensitas watch and increased her consumption of fags to make sure she got through enough by the deadline of 18 April. At the end of February she did a rough calculation and realised that at her present rate she didn't have a snowball's chance in hell of smoking enough to get the watch. Even if she stayed up all night, smoking twenty-four hours a day, she just didn't have the puff to do it. So everyone had to help. My grandfather and grandmother were told to smoke more. Neighbours were asked to contribute. Even my father, who usually smoked Capstan Full Strength or Woodbines, was ordered to swap to Kensitas and at least make a contribution to his own present.

The vouchers were all gathered together in an old shoe box and every Saturday night, while listening to *Saturday Night Theatre* on the Home Service, she would take the box out from under the stairs and count them. I can hear her now, whispering in a hypnotic way which never failed to send me to sleep. Two hundred and twenty five . . . two hundred and twenty six . . . two hundred and twenty seven. . . . Eventually she'd done it. She'd got enough. So on the Sunday morning after the final count she announced to the family that she had achieved her goal and then parcelled up the vouchers ready for sending off to Kensitas first thing on Monday morning.

Ten days later the package arrived. Dad was out, so Mum opened it to inspect the goods. Sure enough, there it was. A crisp leather strap either side of a watch with a luminous dial. Mum was pleased and could hardly wait to show everybody else. Everyone except Dad, of course. He would have to wait until his birthday, which was still a few days away.

But I spoiled it. With the indestructible logic of a child I ruined her day. The sight of the watch brought back to me the months of everyone in the family smoking themselves to death, the anguish of wondering if she would gather together enough vouchers in time and the way she had browbeaten everyone into supporting her cause. All I said was, 'It would've been cheaper just to buy a watch. They've got them like that over the road in Woollies for one pound ten and six.' My mother looked stunned. I felt sorry for her. The look on her face said everything. She had slaved away smoking fag after fag for months. She'd encouraged everybody else to do the same. She'd begged, cajoled, persuaded and bribed friends and neighbours into taking part in her campaign . . . for what? The awful truth suddenly dawned on her. She could have just walked over the road and bought almost the same watch for probably a fraction of what she'd spent on fags. Dad's birthday somehow lost some of its sparkle.

The smokers also, it has to be said, kept the house very clean. I remember my friends' houses were never as clean as ours. And the cause was the smoke. Inside my mother's brain two forces continually vied for supremacy. She had this irresistible urge to smoke for England and yet had a thing about decorating. Whenever she had a free moment she would get out the paintbrush and start painting, and my poor dad never had a minute's peace. If she decided that the house needed decorating she gave him his orders and he, almost without a whimper, put his old clothes on and started stripping the walls. And the connection between the urge to smoke and the urge to decorate? Cause and effect. The acrid smoke of the cigarettes destroyed the paint and wallpaper. That little house was decorated inside from top to bottom every year because the smoke made all the paintwork turn yellow and settled like an oily scum on the walls. So as the seasons changed they were marked by annual rituals reminiscent of primitive tribal rites. Every spring the house was decorated. Summer was a fallow time because the windows and kitchen door could be left open and this would blow most of the smoke outside, over the wall into Mrs Kelsall's back yard. But by October the paintwork and wallpaper needed a good wipe down with a damp cloth and my mother would set about the task with a will.

December was the time when the other source of smoke was seen to. The only source of heat in the whole house was the open fire in the sitting room. On the coldest nights in the dead of winter, when the wind was howling outside or the frost painted beautiful patterns on the windows, the only place to get warm was in front of the living-room fire. The trouble was that with six of us in the house it was difficult even to see the fire, let alone get close enough to it to get warm. And when you did get close enough to feel its warmth it only warmed your front. Your back was still cold and if anybody opened the door an icy blast blew straight in from the North Pole and almost sliced you in half. On the other hand, if the wind was blowing in the right (or wrong, depending on your perception) direction it would come down the chimney and fill the room with dense black smoke, making the whole place smell like Lime Street station before they electrified the railways.

And of course the chimney had to be swept. The responsibility for this fell for some reason on my grandmother. What a major operation it was! The night before the sweep's visit the carpet had to be rolled up and laid on the stairs, and as much furniture as possible had to be carried into the drawing room (the other kids in the neighbourhood all had a front parlour, but in our house it was the drawing room). The bulky sideboard, which looked as if it had been pinched from some monastery, was covered in an enormous white sheet, as were the two big armchairs.

On the appointed day at eight o'clock in the morning the sweep arrived. He was old and covered in soot, even at that time of the morning. In he would trudge, taking care to walk only on the lino or where the newspapers had been strategically positioned to protect the fitted carpet in the hall. As long as he obeyed the rules his life was not in danger. But one foot in the wrong place and . . . !

While he was traipsing through the house with a variety of brushes and rods my grandmother would make a pot of tea. I say 'make' but in fact 'distil' would be a better word. When my friends' mums or nans made tea they simply put tea in the teapot (never without warming it first!) and poured the boiling water on it. But not my nan. Oh no. She poured the boiling water into the pot, yes, but then she would put it on a low light on the stove and let it simmer and bubble and gurgle away for about half an hour. The result was a dense black liquid almost thick enough to stand a spoon up in. Then she poured it into two cups, added two hefty dollops of condensed milk (or 'connie-onnie', as it was universally referred to) and stirred it. Of all the people I remember from my childhood, only the sweep and my nan liked their tea like this.

Once he picked up the cup, that was it. The brushes and rods and cloths just lay on the floor while he and my grandmother chatted. One conversation I remember very well.

'The missus is bad. Gorra growth.'

'Och, the poor soul.'

'Yis. I don't think she's got long to go. Bringin' up all sorts she is. Yells in pain every night. Doctors can't do nottin' for 'er. Father Ryan says it'll be a merciful relief.'

It's all beyond me. The bits I do understand I don't understand. What's wrong with a growth? I thought growth was good. Everyone kept telling me to eat my food so I'd grow. And how could you bring up all sorts? I liked Liquorice All Sorts but once they were down they were down.

Eventually he got on with the job he came to do. He'd cover the grate with a big black cloth and then start feeding the big brush up the chimney, fixing wooden poles on one after another until there were none left. Then I was given the job of going out into the street to see if the brush was poking out of the chimney pot. When it was, Nan gave me sixpence for luck.

The result of all this was two or three sacks of soot which the sweep carried through the kitchen and dumped into his cart. Then he tied all his rods and brushes together, asked for five shillings and was on his way. Before he was at the end of the road Nan would have a bucket, mop and cloth out and start cleaning up all the mess caused by the errant soot as it settled on the floors, windows, walls – everywhere, in fact, that wasn't covered by white cloth.

When the sweep had gone we knew that the cycle of the seasons had been completed. Everywhere now had to be cleaned up, the dust cloths had to be removed and the furniture put back in its proper place, so that we could all settle down and relax until after Christmas. Then, as sure as eggs is eggs, my mother would make plans for the spring clean and start thinking about how she was going to redecorate.

2

Roots

I never knew my grandparents on my father's side. His mother had died when he was only seven and his father died not long after I was born. My grandparents on my mother's side, or Nan and Granddad, as I always called them, were Scots. He was born John Scott Guthrie in Leith near Edinburgh in 1884 but grew up on a croft in the Orkney Isles where his father eked out a living as a carter. Then, in about 1900, he moved back to Edinburgh where he met my grandmother and they were married in 1909. When he landed a job as a shipping clerk (because of his fine penmanship, he always said) they moved down to Liverpool just before the First World War and spent the rest of their lives there.

Peter Guthrie, the author's great-grandfather on his mother's side, a native Orcadian. This photograph was taken on the Orkneys in about 1890. *(Author's collection)*

John Scott Guthrie, the author's grandfather, early 1900s. *(Author's collection)*

Now John Guthrie was almost a caricature of your dour Scotsman. Not very tall, he was none the less powerfully built and in his youth was no mean footballer. He used to kid my sister and me that when he was a young man football clubs were queuing up all over the place to sign him up but he refused them all because although he was good at the game he was too attached to his knees. It was OK to play a game on a Saturday morning, but enough was enough and he did not want to be crippled with arthritis in the knees by the age of thirty, which was what happened to many of his friends who played a lot of football.

Granddad stayed in the shipping business all his life and always caught the five to eight train from the Black Bull station in the morning to take him to his office, which had transferred to Manchester during the war. He wore a businessman's suit with a waistcoat and silver watch-chain, horn-rimmed spectacles and a trilby. But he always wore black boots. Even when he wore a suit I don't ever remember him wearing shoes, but I would watch, absolutely fascinated, every night as he sat down in his armchair and unlaced his highly polished black-leather boots, pulled them off and placed them carefully in the corner by the chimney breast. Then he would put his slippers on and remove his collar and tie. In those days men wore detachable collars and Granddad was no exception.

There was a special drawer in the sideboard where he kept his clean collars, together with a small box in which he had a variety of front studs, back studs and cufflinks. Nobody was allowed to go in that drawer. It was only opened when my grandfather wanted to take out a clean collar, except for Thursdays. My grandmother never cleaned his collars. That job was done by a specialist laundry in the centre of Liverpool called Collars. Every Thursday a van would turn up outside the front door and the driver would deliver a small brown cardboard box containing six gleaming starched collars and take away six dirty ones, to be returned the following week all bright, white and gleaming. Another box which used to turn up, but not with the same degree of regularity, was also made of brown cardboard, but the greasy stain on the outside and unpleasant smell that came from the inside announced contents of a very different kind . . . kippers. To this day I don't know why or how, but my grandfather managed somehow, when rationing was still on, to have Manx kippers delivered to the door. As a child I soon learned to distinguish kippers from collars.

The Black Bull pub in Aintree, at the junction of Longmoor Lane and Warbreck Moor. (*Liverpool Record Office*)

When he retired in the early 1950s he took on the duty of going to fetch the *Liverpool Echo*. Morning papers such as The *News Chronicle* and The *Daily Express* and a deluge of Sunday papers were delivered by the local newsagent. But not the *Echo*. Oh no. The *Echo* was special and had to be fetched every evening; it was my grandfather who always undertook this arduous task. Hail, rain or shine, he insisted that it was his duty to venture forth from the comfort of the family home and return with his quarry some considerable time later. The significance of the paper-boy's stand being right outside the Black Bull totally escaped me at the time. But, even though I was a child, it did occur to me that an hour and a half to run an errand which really should have only taken about ten minutes seemed excessive. And I suppose I must have been about eight or nine when I noticed that on his return there was a different smell about him. When he went out there was nothing more unusual than the smell of the ancient mothball that hung next to his jacket in the hall wardrobe. But when he returned with the evening paper he always smelled the way my father smelled after drinking the contents of a certain brown bottle with

The original Windsor Castle at the junction of Orrell Lane and Walton Vale. It was destroyed by a parachute bomb in the war and rebuilt in the 1950s. This photograph was taken in 1904. *(Liverpool Record Office)*

his Sunday dinner. As part of the process of growing up I came to associate that smell with what Dad called his 'special lemonade' but the label on the bottle called 'Light Ale'.

Once he was back in the house my grandfather's routine was always the same. He would throw the *Echo* on to his armchair in the corner of the sitting room and, no matter how eager anyone else was to read it, the unspoken law was that he had first claim on it. While he was in the hall taking off his coat and hanging it carefully in the wardrobe, the virginal rolled-up broadsheet lay where it had landed and slowly uncurled as the heat from the coal fire reached it. Not even my grandmother, who was by no stretch of the imagination a timid woman or doormat of a wife, and was always eager to read the horse-racing results, dared to pick it up before her turn.

Slippers on, collar and tie off, specs perched on the end of his nose, Granddad would give a slight cough, fold the paper into a shape more comfortable for reading, and that was it. That moment was the signal that the evening had begun. The tea dishes would have been washed by now ('dinner' was the meal we had at two o'clock on Sundays and on Christmas Day), the Home Service had been tuned in for the news, another shovel-full of coal had been heaped on to the fire (or, as my grandmother used to say, the fire had been 'backed up') and everyone was seized by a ritual fit of generosity as friendly arguments broke out over who should accept whose cigarettes.

My grandfather, then, would sit in the corner of the room, peering through his horn-rimmed spectacles and systematically ploughing through the *Echo* while other members of the family smoked and engaged in what always seemed to me to be incomprehensible and meaningless conversation. Now and again my sister Margaret would talk about a film she had seen at the Palace, the Carlton or the Walton Vale, and she and my mother would discuss the relative sexual attractions exuded by a variety of male film stars. Not that the word 'sex' ever crossed their lips and it was only years later that I came to understand that this, in fact, was what was being discussed. By common consent it was usually agreed by the end of these conversations that Clark Gable (or 'Big Ears', as my mother always referred to him) was more handsome than James Stewart or Errol Flynn.

When my father looked at the *Echo* he always turned first to the sports section. He, like my grandfather, had been a useful man on the field in his day, and he cherished a life-long passion for the game and his team (Liverpool, of course). This meant that he never missed a match if he could help it or the opportunity to read about one. If his team was playing well he would engage in 'discussions' with my grandfather, a keen Everton supporter whose impish sense of fun goaded him into making uncomplimentary remarks about Billy Liddell or Albert Stubbins, just to needle Dad. It has to be said, though, that these 'discussions' never got out of hand or could ever be described as being anything other than just friendly banter. Yes, there was rivalry between them, but it never stopped them going off to the match together on Saturdays to support whichever team was playing at home that week, or analysing the game the same night in the Queen's Arms or the Sefton. Later on, when the Windsor Castle, the pub at the junction of Rice Lane and Orrell Lane

The rebuilt Windsor Castle pub, 1970s. *(Liverpool Record Office)*

(destroyed in the war), was rebuilt in about 1954, it became their regular Saturday-night venue for reliving the day's match and comparing the players of the day with the pre-war greats.

I don't remember how long the Home Service programmes lasted, but I do remember that they seemed to go on and on about things I could not understand and which seemed singularly uninteresting to me. I do have a clear memory, however, of how the announcer's voice would sometimes fade so that my grandfather had to lean over in his chair and attempt to tune the station in again. At such moments all conversation would cease as Granddad put his ear hard up against the radio while simultaneously fiddling with the knob. The silence that accompanied these antics was frequently interrupted by the sound of a tram passing at the end of the road, much to my grandfather's annoyance and interrupting his concentration. When this delicate operation eventually proved successful there would be a collective sigh of relief and the chatter would be resumed. My child's mind could never understand why the family conversations were always loudest when the radio was working well and the reception was good, as it always seemed to me that the best time to talk was when no sound was coming out of the radio. But the logic of a child is seldom the logic of the adult world.

At what I suppose would have been about seven thirty the Home Service was abandoned and it was time to tune into the Light Programme. If my memory serves me right Tuesday night was when we listened to *Have a Go*, introduced by Wilfred Pickles with Mabel at the piano. On Friday nights it was *Take it From Here*, with Jimmy Edwards and his interminable saga 'The Glums', with Ron and Eth. As we got older my sister and I used to ask for Radio Luxembourg and, strangely enough, we were often supported in our request by Granddad, especially when Winifred Atwell was on. No musician himself, his fingers would nevertheless tap away on the arm of his chair in time with her inimitable style. But my abiding memory is not her dexterity at the keyboard, but the sponsor's name, Horace Batchelor, read out at the end of every programme and the town where the main office was based which was spelled out letter by letter – K E Y N S H A M. This should, I suppose, tell us something about the power of advertising!

By this time the *Echo* had usually been dismembered and everyone in the family had claimed the pages he or she was particularly interested in. For my mother and sister it was the horoscope. My grandmother devoured the horse-racing page as she studied the form and my father got to grips with the crossword. As I trotted off to bed and turned to say 'goodnight' I little thought that the image of him, with his newly acquired retractable ballpoint pen poised over something as ephemeral as that evening's edition of the *Echo*, would bring back such vivid memories fifty-odd years later.

3

The Sport of Kings

Then there was Nan. What a woman she was! Peggy Guthrie, 4ft 10 in her shoes, dominated the household for much of my childhood. She was born in 1885 in Edinburgh, the daughter of Alexander Robertson, who owned a tailoring business near the centre of the city. At the age of about thirteen she was taken out of school and put to work learning to become a seamstress alongside, as she always put it, Germans, Jews and Russians (although she always pronounced it Rooshians). And this training stood her in good stead for later life, as she went on to bring up four children and made all their clothing. She also learned a smattering of her workmates' languages. Well into her seventies and eighties she could still recall phrases in Russian, German and Yiddish, and I have a theory that she was probably a gifted linguist at heart but just never had the opportunity to develop her talent.

Nan looked after my sister and me a great deal when we were very young. Mum, Dad and Granddad all left the house early in the morning to go off to their jobs, and my sister, seven years older than myself, would leave the house not much later to go to school. Then, until I started school too, I would come downstairs in my pyjamas and Nan would look after me for the rest of the day.

Dark winter mornings I loved. Even now, when I think back, a warm glow flows through my veins when I remember how she would have a lovely roaring fire dancing in the grate and my clothes all laid out in a neat row on the hearth. I would sit on a little stool by the fire eating toast dripping with butter and drinking lovely hot milk. Then there would be as much of a strange substance called calf's-foot jelly as I could eat and which, Nan promised, was very good for me and would make me big and strong.

Breakfast over, she would bring in a bowl of warm soapy water and give me a good wash before dressing me. What a palaver dressing was! There seemed to be layers and layers of clothes: vest (or singlet, as Nan always called it), liberty bodice (does anybody else remember them?), shirt and pullover above the waist. The area below the waist, by comparison, was neglected. A pair of underpants and then short trousers. The result was that when I went out to play the top half was warm but the bottom half froze. My knees in the winter were always red and chapped with the wind and the rain; it never seemed to occur to anyone that some article of clothing designed to cover up the part between the hem of the short trousers and top of the socks could have been beneficial. Long trousers for boys were only invented in the late fifties or early sixties.

Margaret (Peggy) Guthrie, the author's grandmother, photographed in the early 1900s. (*Author's collection*)

Nan lived in Liverpool for over seventy years but her heart was always back home in Edinburgh, or Auld Reekie as she always called it. And she never lost her broad Scots accent, which caused problems at times. I had no problem understanding either of my grandparents and don't remember ever being conscious of their different way of pronouncing words. All my friends had Scouse accents and when they came to see me there were frequent scenes of mutual incomprehension between them and my grandparents. They really could not understand each other and I remember, even before I started school, I often had to act as an interpreter so that they could communicate.

But my linguistic skills were not perfect. Spending most of the time with my grandparents meant that I spoke a kind of hybrid Scots Scouse or Scouse Scots dialect and more than once got them confused. One day my grandfather said to me 'Cm'eer, son, away up tae the shop fr'a' poond o' treckle tawffee.'

So off I go and walk into the shop and say to the lady behind the counter, 'Ma granfaither's wantin' a poond o' treckle tawffee.'

She looked bemused and said 'Y'wa, lad?'

I repeat the request and again the lady has extreme difficulty coping with the linguistic problem I have set her. Then another customer comes to her aid, 'It's awrright. Dat's Mrs Guthrie's grandson. 'Ee's axin' yer for treeckle toffeee. Dat over der's what ee wants.'

As soon as it was safe enough to let me out on to the streets alone there was another errand I ran almost every day. My grandmother, good as she was at looking after me, had two weaknesses. One of them was the horses. Every morning at about ten o'clock she would make herself a witches' brew of that dreadful concoction she called tea. Next she would light a fag and study the racing pages of the *News Chronicle*. Then, very carefully, she would do some writing on a bluish piece of paper, fold it neatly, put it in an envelope with a five shilling postal order and seal it. 'Wee Al,' she would then call. 'Ma letter's ready fer ma solicitor', and off I would go to the post office by the Black Bull and post it.

Her 'solicitor' was someone in Glasgow called Johnnie McLoughlin. But he wasn't a solicitor at all; he was a bookie. Why she had to send her bets off to Glasgow every day I haven't a clue, but it must have had something to do with the gaming laws of the time. And even after betting shops opened in the 1960s she still used her Glasgow office; then when I started school our kind-hearted milkman got the job of making sure that that brown envelope was in the box in time for the 11.30 a.m. collection.

But I have a terrible tale to tell about Johnnie McLoughlin. From the age of about six, on Saturdays and during the school holidays I always assumed the responsibility of making sure her letter was posted in time to arrive in Glasgow by first post the next working day. No matter what the weather I would make my way along Walton Vale, past the cinema and the Methodist church, resisting the temptation to call in at the sweets and tobacconist's shop and never being deflected from my mission. Not once.

When I was about fifteen I was still faithfully carrying out this solemn duty. But one day everything went wrong. Badly wrong. About as seriously badly wrong as it is possible for things to go.

About four o'clock one Saturday afternoon I'm standing in the kitchen talking to my father and just happen to slide my hand into my jacket pocket. My hand brushes against something that feels uncannily like an envelope. I pull it out and my heart stops.

'Oh God,' I say, 'I've forgotten to post Nan's letter.'

'Never mind,' Dad says. 'You've probably saved her some money. She's had a run of bad luck recently. Don't say anything till after the last race. It'll be OK.'

The words are hardly out of his mouth when the door bursts open. Nan's standing there, shaking with excitement, the colour drained from her face. 'I've won,' she says. 'I've won a Yankee. Thirrty poonds.'

I just wanted to die and be roasted in hell for all eternity. I had been rushing for a bus to go and meet some friends and when I saw it coming over the railway bridge I dashed to the bus stop and, for the first time in my life, forgot to post that blasted letter.

I did not have the heart to tell her. To this day I still cringe when I think of the moment – the moment when I showed my true colours as a squirming, slithering, slippery, slimy coward and let Dad do the explaining. Nan's knees buckled. She gasped, muttered something about her Creator, grabbed hold of the door handle with her bony hand and held on like grim death so as not to collapse in an amorphous heap on the floor. Never before in the history of the turf had such a catastrophe been suffered by one punter! In fifty years of betting on the gee-gees she had never won more than a couple of quid, so £30 was a fortune. To give some idea of the enormity of the loss I will just say that when I started my career as a graduate teacher almost ten years after this incident I started on £18 per week. You could do a helluva lot with £30 in 1959.

My ignorance of sport is encyclopaedic. I have never been interested in it and I think this has a lot to do with the family I was born into, and particularly with Saturday afternoons. Football dominated most of the male conversation in the house, and the combination of football and horse racing made Saturdays a nightmare. From my early teens I would leave the house on a Saturday morning as early as possible and only return briefly in the evening in time to have a bite to eat and then get ready to go out.

It was like this. I'd get up at about nine o'clock and go downstairs for some breakfast. These were the days when lots of people, including Mum and Dad, had to work a half-day on Saturday, so by that time of the morning there would only be my grandparents and me in the house (my sister got married when I was fourteen and left the nest to live in married bliss at the end of the earth – some blasted heath called Ormskirk).

When I'd finished my breakfast I'd go into the sitting room. Nan would be sitting in her armchair, bent almost double reading the racing pages with a magnifying glass.

'I'll no' be a minute, son', she would say ritualistically, painstakingly continuing to write out her bets as she spoke, and never failing to add, 'if I win taeday I'll see ye dinna go short.' And to give credit where credit's due, if she won there was always a couple of shillings in it for me. The trouble is, she hardly ever won and was the living proof of one of my grandfather's favourite sayings: 'There's only one winner and that's the bookie.'

By this time the room was already filling with smoke. She would have been sitting there since about half past eight and was probably already on her fourth or fifth fag of the day. It was time for me to go. As soon as she'd written her 'letter to her solicitor' I would take hold of it and disappear. I knew only too well what it would be like if I didn't. The fug would just get thicker and thicker as the sun outside got higher and higher.

Speaking on Saturday afternoons was almost a hanging offence. Nan would listen to the racing on the radio from about one o'clock and only someone with a death wish would have dared to speak when she was listening to a race. Then Granddad would come home from the football match with Dad and he'd want to listen to anything on the radio about football. And then it was six o'clock. God help anyone who even breathed! Six o'clock was *Sports Report* and he would sit at the table and write down all the results as they were read out over the air. I can hear the dark brown voice even now: 'Everton 1, Sheffield Wednesday 3; Arsenal 5, Charlton Athletic 2.' This was followed by the results from Scotland: 'Heart of Midlothian 3, Stenhousemuir 2; Arbroath nil, Hibernians 2', etc., etc. Any interruption was greeted with a loud 'Shshsh' and a look that could strip paint off woodwork.

Granddad died in 1958. We got a television in 1959. Then Saturdays got even worse. From midday there was horse racing, football, horse racing again, then more football on the screen. Nan watched the lot. So did Dad after a few lunchtime pints in the Windsor Castle. Out came the fags. The curtains were drawn so that the old black-and-white picture was easier to see. When Uncle Alex was home on leave even more fags were smoked but he added an extra element: a bottle of gin. The room was transformed into a den of iniquity where if you liked sport, fags and booze you were in, if you didn't you were out. And I was definitely out. I hated it and have disliked sport and anything to do with sport intensely ever since.

I said Nan had two weaknesses. One was the horses, the other was whisky. Granddad liked his beer and the occasional 'wee drachm' (he always pronounced the 'ch' as in 'loch') but he knew when to say no. By no stretch of the imagination could it ever be said that he drank too much or too often. But Nan? She almost bathed in it. Somehow my mother kept Nan's fondness for the hard stuff hidden from friends and relatives. Believe it or not, I was in my early teens before I knew she was a drinker, but by that time she was drinking so much it was impossible to hide it from anyone.

The secret revealed itself to me one day when I came home from school. It was about five o'clock on a freezing November evening a few weeks after Granddad died, and a thick pea-souper hung like a shroud over the whole of Aintree. The first thing I noticed as I approached the front door was that there were no lights on in the house. That was odd, very odd. There was always somebody in at that time. Then when I went to put my key in the door I found that it was already open. The scene was like something out of a thriller or one of those dreadful mystery films I used to go and watch at the Walton Vale picture-house on Saturday afternoons when I was about seven or eight. I pushed the door open and walked in. The fog drifted in from the street and mingled with the pitch dark of the long, narrow hall. I started to move gingerly towards where I knew the light switch was and then fell over something bulky in the middle of the floor. I picked myself up, groped my way along the wall to the switch and switched the light on.

When I turned round I saw that the bulky object on the floor was Nan. She still had her outdoor hat and coat on, and my first assumption was that she'd been out somewhere, come home and had either just fainted or had a heart attack and died. But when I got closer I soon realised what was wrong. She was drunk. I hadn't noticed it until then, but suddenly I became aware of the smell of whisky hovering in the hall, and the closer I got to Nan the stronger the smell got. She was magnificently, stupendously, gloriously smashed. What was I to do? Through my adolescent mind flashed an image of myself on the screen at the Walton Vale. I was the hero. I knew what Clark Gable would have done. He'd have just picked her up in his brawny, virile arms, carried her upstairs and dropped her on the bed. So that's exactly what I did.

As I was walking downstairs, feeling all grown up and fully in control of the situation, I heard her call out, 'Wee Al, bring me ma drink.' I knew she meant whisky but I took her a glass of water. She was neither pleased nor displeased at my beneficence. By the time I got back with it she was dead to the world.

4

Many Are Cold,
but Few Are Frozen

D oes anyone know where Siberia is?' asked Mr Lamden. Nobody answered. Colin Morgan, the class brainbox who later got a scholarship to Cambridge, stayed quiet. So did Ian Hay, another bright spark. And when Ian Coulthard couldn't answer either I thought this was my chance for glory. I knew where it was. My grandfather always referred to the outside lav as Siberia because it was so cold there.

So up shot my hand. Mr Lamden smiled in amazement at the thought of my knowing something nobody else in the class knew.

'Please sir, it's on the other side of our back yard.'

'What?'

'On the other side of our back yard, sir. Our outside lav's Siberia.'

Mr Lamden burst out laughing. Colin Morgan, Ian Hay and Ian Coulthard followed, and then the whole class joined in. I sank further and further back into my seat and blushed with embarrassment. That cured me. I decided I would never answer a question in Mr Lamden's class again and I don't think I ever did. In fact, until I left Rice Lane Junior School in 1955 I don't think I ever risked exposing myself to ridicule again by attempting to answer a teacher's question.

The outside toilet (actually we did not have toilets in Liverpool, we only had 'lavs') was a testament to and symbol of the hardiness of our family. We had a toilet upstairs too, but the unwritten law of the house, laid down by my mother, was that you could only use it if you were already upstairs. It was strictly forbidden for anyone to go upstairs just to use the lav. And this law was decreed for one reason and one reason only: to protect the stair carpet. My mother had spent what in those days was an astronomical amount on carpets for the hall and stairs, and she wanted them to last long enough to see her out. She knew there wasn't much she could do about the hall carpet, but it was possible to restrict the wear and tear on the stairs, and so we all had to use the outside lav as much as possible. In summer there was no problem, but winter! Jesus, it was cold in winter!

Let me describe the scene. It's January and the temperature is well below freezing. You need to go to the lav but you can't hang on until bedtime so you can't go upstairs. When you've got to go you've got to go. So you open the back kitchen

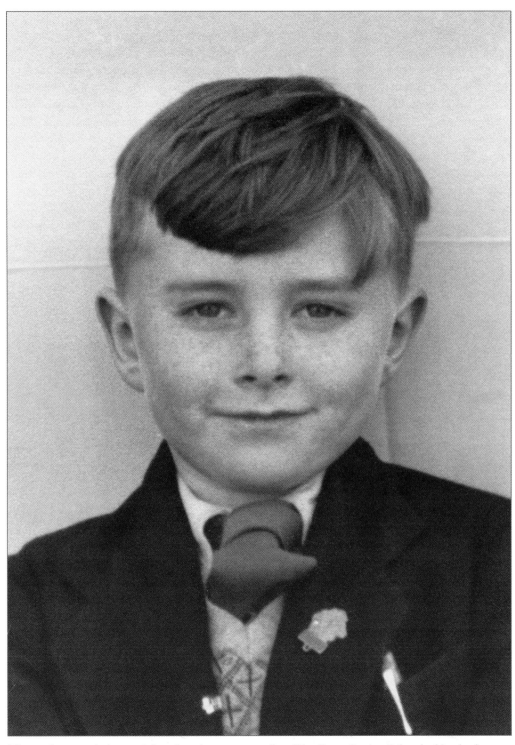

The author aged about eight when he was a pupil at Rice Lane Junior School. *(Author's collection)*

door and there's a blizzard blowing. Suddenly you're Scott of the Antarctic and you start plodding through six inches of snow to reach your destination. When you get there the latch on the lav door is frozen solid and it's pitch dark so you have to do everything by feel. You kick the door. You bang on the latch, all the time feeling that if the door doesn't open you just do it there where you're standing and to hell with it. But then there's a clicking sound and the door opens. Inside it's still pitch black and there's no light in there. You're totally blind and experience alone guides you so that you know how many steps to take before you're in position for whatever function you've gone there to perform. If it's a stand-up job there's no problem. You just wait for the sound of water landing on water (or more probably ice) and then, when it stops, you turn round and retrace your steps. Back into the snow, making sure you've buttoned your flies up well so there's no danger of frost-bite!

But sitting down out there was something that has to be experienced to be believed. The wooden seat is almost certainly covered with frost. You sit in the dark for as long as it takes. You think of anything to take your mind off the biting cold that makes your teeth chatter and almost freezes your bum to the seat. Then you try to pull the chain. It's frozen. It can't be flushed until tomorrow when, you hope, the temperature rises above zero and the water will flow again. No wonder I thought I knew the answer to Mr Lamden's question.

Not that the inside of the house was all that much warmer. Yes, the sitting room (usually referred to as the 'front room', which was rather illogical as it was at the back of the house) was relatively warm because of the coal fire. But there was never any heating, even in the dead of winter, in any other room in the whole house. The real front room (always called the drawing room at my grandmother's insistence) had an electric fire but nobody was ever allowed to use it because of the terrible cost of electricity. As a consequence the room was virtually unused. There were only three reasons for anyone being allowed in there. Either it was Christmas Day or we had visitors who were entertained in there or someone was dead. On Christmas Day and the rare occasion when we had visitors (they were not encouraged) Mum relaxed and allowed the electric fire to be switched on for a couple of hours. But only one bar, mind. When someone died the coffin was put in there for a few hours before the undertakers came to convey it to the crematorium. On those days the fire was not allowed to be switched on as the dead don't feel the cold and (God help me for saying it) they were going to get a good warming soon enough anyway.

But the cold in the pretentiously named drawing room was not just physical. An eerie, almost sepulchral chill resided in that room. It was beautifully furnished with a sumptuous three-piece suite, a charming little oak coffee table and a genuine Persian carpet on the floor. These personal effects might sound totally incongruous in a little terraced house in a working-class district of Liverpool, but none of them had been bought; the family could never have afforded such quality. No, they were all prizes Nan had won in the 1930s and '40s when she was a champion player at ladies' bowls. But these luxuries were never used. In the twenty years I spent in that house the room probably never had more than a total of a few hours' use or heat. Dad used to refer to it as the 'inner sanctum', and it had a feel of the grave about it that never left it. Even years later, when I had left home, married and had children of my own, on return visits I still felt uneasy walking into that room.

Upstairs it was even colder. In two of the bedrooms, mine being one of them, the windows would not shut properly and so the air blew in one and out of the other all the time. In summer it was pleasant, but in winter it meant that a constant icy blast blew from the front of the house to the back. I could lie in my bed and feel the icy wind blowing over my face, and in moments of boredom if I couldn't get to sleep I could literally stretch my arm out and scratch the ice off the inside of the window.

Not that it ever bothered me. I never even thought about it. That's just the way things were and it's only with hindsight, from the comfort of a fully centrally heated, double-glazed study, that I can appreciate the difference between then and now. Yes, it was cold. Right up to the day I left home to go to university in 1962 I would get up in the winter and stand on freezing lino, put freezing clothes on and thought nothing of seeing the cold air hovering in my bedroom or my breath turn almost into droplets of ice as it left my mouth.

And yet it doesn't seem to have done us any harm. In fact I can honestly say that I hardly ever remember any member of the family being ill. Nobody seemed to catch flu. I don't ever remember my mother or father having even a day off work through illness.

I don't think they ever even caught a cold.

5

Brotherly Love

I was a real pest to my sister. With her blonde hair and chubby little face everyone thought she was a regular little Shirley Temple. And this perception of her was reinforced by the fact that she was into dancing in a big way. She attended Mrs Sheila Wyn-Little's tap-dancing class somewhere near Evered Avenue library and plagued the life out of me with her impromptu demonstrations of toe steps, shuffles and American rolls and God knows what other arcane contortions that just left me cold. She thought she was Betty Grable or Rita Hayworth and, at the drop of a hat, she'd go over to the corner and start doing strange things with her feet . . . tap . . . tap . . . tappity tap . . . on the lino then everyone would clap and say what a pretty girl she was. Everyone except me. I could not see what there was to cheer about. After all, it wasn't like watching Tom Mix or Roy Rogers at the Walton Vale in a fight with the baddies or rescuing Dale Evans or some other lissom female from the Injuns. Now that was something to cheer about. But tap dancing?

But she didn't give up easily. Oh no. She was determined to make me appreciate the finer, cultural side of Scouse life, and her preferred technique was the sneaky ambush. She knew where to catch me at my most vulnerable, and when I was sitting on the lav (inside or outside) she would kick the door open and start running through her dance routine in front of me. And she'd provide her own musical accompaniment as well singing la-lala-la-la . . . I could do nothing. The door was too far away for me to reach and if I told her to go away she just sang louder and twirled and tapped even faster, so these ad hoc exhibitions became one of my first lessons in patience. I just stared blankly at her, didn't smile and didn't clap.

'Oh, you!' she'd say, 'you're horrible.'

Then she would stamp her foot, turn round and disappear.

But things got really interesting when she discovered boys. I'm convinced that little brothers are put on this earth for the sole purpose of disrupting their elder sisters' courting. And I have to admit that this was a biological duty that I assumed with alacrity. There is no greater buzz than the reaction you get pulling faces at your big sister's boyfriend when he thinks he's on a promise for a bit of a snog. It's even more fun than messing things up for your sister when she trying to get out for a date, as I did one day with spectacular results in Llandudno.

Llandudno was where we always went for our holidays. We couldn't afford a holiday every year and when we did go away it was never for more than a week. Well, one year in the late forties or early fifties we had made our way to Mrs Jones's

The author's sister Margaret, in 1940 when she was three years old. *(Author's collection)*

cottage at the foot of the Great Orme. A few years later, when family finances must have improved a little, we would stay in the Craig-Ard hotel near the beach, but until then it was always Mrs Jones's.

On this particular occasion Marg (as she was generally known) had met some lad who wanted to take her on a date to the pictures or a dance, I don't remember which exactly. Unfortunately for her, the date coincided with my parents' attempts at converting me into something resembling a socially acceptable, well-mannered little boy. I was constantly being told not to pick my nose, not to stare at other people and not to interrupt them when they were speaking. The lesson of the week in Llandudno was that it was bad manners to leave the table before everyone had finished eating. What a gift! What a wonderful new tool in my box of tricks for annoying my sister!

There we all were around the table having our evening meal. My mother and sister were just about to start clearing away the dishes when I said, 'I haven't finished yet, and you said it's bad manners to leave the table before everyone's finished.'

Mum looked at Dad and they knew there was nothing they could do. How could they not obey the social conventions they were trying to get me to abide by? So they just had to sit there, patiently, silently.

But my sister was furious. She still had to add the finishing touches to her make-up and then get down into the town to meet her new gentleman friend.

'I'll just have another piece of cake,' I said, 'and can I have another drink, please?'

Marg was getting agitated.

'Oh, Mum,' she said, 'he's just doing this to make me late.'

'You'll have to wait,' was the reply. 'We've all got to wait till he's finished.'

The feeling of power was intoxicating. I spent ages eating that piece of cake. It was beautiful and light and just melted in your mouth, but I made it last and last, swirling it around my mouth and squeezing it between my teeth, time and time again, before swallowing each morsel. Then I'd go through the same process again with the next tiny morsel until eventually I could not stretch things out any more and I had to let the last mouthful slide down my throat. Then I said I'd just have one more scone. When that had disappeared at the same protractedly slow pace I thought I could manage just one more. After that I noticed there was still some bread left on the plate in the middle of the table so I started finishing that off as well. By now I was stuffed. I really felt as though I would explode at any moment but I fought valiantly to overcome the sensations of satiety and crammed every last crumb into my mouth. My sister meanwhile was progressing through all the negative emotions it is possible for a human being to experience. First it was annoyance, then frustration, followed by white-hot anger and then, close on its heels, came murderous intent.

I knew when to stop. After all, if she throttled me I would never be able to repeat the exercise, so I gave in, admitted defeat and slid off the chair and flopped full stretch on the settee. A few minutes later the room started swimming and I broke out into a sweat and began to experience that awful feeling that tells you you're going to be sick and there's nothing you can do to keep it down. I just got to the grid outside in time. I felt dreadful. One half of me thought I was going to die and the other half hoped I would. But Marg missed her date. I had made her late and her friend didn't wait. I had a victory. A pyrrhic victory but it was a victory none the less. Aren't little brothers horrible?

In her mid-teens my sister's interest in dancing expanded to include the ballroom variety. She changed her allegiance from Mrs Wyn-Little's and enrolled as a student with Thompson's School of Dancing at the top of Melling Road and just a stone's throw away from Aintree Racecourse.

Her talent and enthusiasm for ballroom dancing were no less powerful than for tap. My memory of it is that several times a week she would come home from work (she was a shorthand typist at Jacobs biscuit factory), gobble her tea, dash upstairs and get ready. An hour later we would just hear 'Going out . . . Bye . . .' and the

The Promenade at Llandudno, which became a popular seaside resort in the mid-nineteenth century. *(Jim Roberts)*

front door would slam and that was it. I wouldn't see her again until the next morning.

Occasionally, very occasionally (probably no more than once a year), Mum and Dad would go out together for the evening. When this happened the grandparents took on the role of seeing to it that Marg and I got a meal. But there was one time (and I think it happened only once during the whole time I lived in Grace Road) when Mum and Dad had to go off somewhere and Nan and Granddad were also out. So Mum delegated. Marg was to give me my tea. But Marg wanted to go out dancing, didn't she?

Now when I was a kid there was nothing in the whole wide world I hated more than onions. I couldn't stand the smell or taste of them raw, but boiled they were the greatest abomination in the whole of Creation. The slippery, slimy feel of them in your mouth made you think of worms and I detested them. The Sunday School teacher told us that God created the world and all that was in it and it was God who gave us the food that landed on our tables every day. Bread, meat, fruit I could understand. But onions? Never. God could not have created such a revolting vegetable as that and still have been called beneficent or benevolent. Only a

A distant view of Llandudno's pier. (*Jim Roberts*)

malicious deity could have come up with such a terrible formula for a vegetable. It must have been created by the devil.

And my sister, along with everyone else in the house, knew of my detestation of the repellent, supposedly edible bulb. But what was placed in front of me on that memorable night when she was charged with giving me a meal? An onion. A whole, boiled, gleaming, slippery onion with a knob of butter on top. Nothing else. That was all there was on the plate.

'You know I hate onions,' I protested.

She was already dressed in her finery and ready to go out to Thompson's School of Dancing.

'Do you?' she answered. 'I thought you liked them. Bye . . .'. And the front door slammed shut.

That was the night I discovered just how long it takes to cut a boiled onion into pieces small enough to fit down the plug-hole of a kitchen sink.

But I had my revenge. And I got the idea of how I was going to get my own back on my sister from the Children's Matinée at the Walton Vale picture-house. The matinées (or 'kids' crushes', as we always called them) were on every Saturday afternoon and I would go with Ray Dowling, Phil Fisher and other assorted kids from the neighbourhood. For a few pennies we could sit and watch the Three Stooges, Flash Gordon or a selection of cartoons followed by the 'feature film' which, nine times out of ten, was a 'cowie', Liverpool dialect for a cowboy film or Western. We would cheer the Lone Ranger, Gene Autry (the Singing Cowboy) and Roy Rogers and then boo the cattle rustlers, Injuns, bank robbers or whoever that week's miscreants happened to be.

On one of these sessions of highbrow entertainment I saw somebody (I can't remember if it was a Laurel and Hardy or an Abbott and Costello prank) tie a piece of cotton to a vase, go outside the room and pull on the cotton. The vase appeared to move of its own accord, to the amazement of the people standing in the room. It occurred to me that, with some minor changes of detail, this had the makings of an excellent practical joke.

Haulfre Gardens, Llandudno, *c.* 1938. It was the favourite place for the author's parents for morning coffee during family holidays in Llandudno. The author preferred an ice-cream sundae! (*Jim Roberts*)

The terminus and ticket office for the Great Orme tram. Mrs Jones's cottage was just behind the hotel, part of whose roof can be glimpsed on the left. (*Jim Roberts*)

So when I got back home the first thing I did was make sure that my sister was still out. She was. I made a beeline for my mother's sewing box and selected a reel of thread which was roughly the same colour as the reddish lino on the floor of my sister's bedroom. Then I crept upstairs, tied the thread to the bottom of a leg of the high-back chair at the foot of her bed and unwound as much thread as was needed for it to stretch into my grandparents' bedroom next door. Then I left it and went downstairs, nonchalantly walked into the sitting room where Nan was listening to the races and sat down. Mum was in the kitchen cooking something for tea and Dad and Granddad still hadn't come back from the match. At about five o'clock Marg came home. The first thing she did was come into the sitting room to feel the side of the chimney breast to see if there was enough hot water for a bath. It didn't feel very warm so she asked Nan to draw the damper as this would heat the water faster.

I was bursting with excitement. I could hardly wait. I was laughing inside at the thought of how she would react to my fiendish plan. I started whistling and drumming like Granddad on the side of the chair to relieve the tension. She looked at me as if I wasn't right in the head, went back into the kitchen and started talking to Mum about something and nothing. About twenty minutes later I heard her go upstairs. Still I waited. After a few minutes I heard one door open and another close. Then there was the sound of running water and I knew she was getting into the bath. This was my moment to move. I stood up, walked out as casually as I could manage, and crept very quietly upstairs so Mum wouldn't hear me wearing out the stair carpet. Once on the landing I tip-toed into Nan and Granddad's room and sat down behind the door. I waited for what seemed like an age. Marg was languishing in the bath singing 'Shrimpboats are a-comin, they're sailing tonight. . . .'

Eventually she pulled the plug and I could hear the water draining away. A minute or two later the bathroom door opened and I heard her skipping along the landing into her bedroom. I waited.

She's still singing when I decide it's zero hour. At first I give the cotton just one quick pull and the singing stops. Then it starts again and I wait again. Another pull is followed by another hiatus in the melodic tones emanating from the bedroom. Now it's time to go for broke so I give the cotton one almighty pull and all hell breaks loose. My sister screams and rushes out on to the landing in a fit of hysteria. Mum comes running up the stairs thinking something terrible has happened to her. Then she sees me. Marg tells her about the moving chair. Mum puts two and two together and makes four, turns and lands what she called a sallywanger, but most people call a slap, on the back of my head.

That night, lying in bed, I've got a thumping headache but still can't stop giggling to myself. The sallywanger was a price well worth paying for giving my sister such a fright.

6

Sunday Observance

Sundays sounded different. They also smelled different. From Monday to Saturday I was awakened at about 6 a.m. by the sound of my grandfather moving about. In my early childhood this was the time when he would be up and getting ready to go to work. But habits of a lifetime are difficult to break and so, even after he retired, he still got up at the same time and would potter about making tea for everyone else, shaving in the kitchen and then reading the morning paper. But on Sundays it was different. Everyone had a lie-in.

On weekdays, as soon as I opened my eyes to the sounds inside the house I also became aware of the sounds outside. Buses and trams I remember in particular. Hundreds of them. Private cars were still a bit of a rarity in the fifties and the vast majority of the populace went to work by public transport. This meant that main roads such as Walton Vale, less than a hundred yards from our front door, roared, hummed and rattled as buses, lorries and tramcars shunted people and goods back and forth all day long. And let's not forget the horse and cart. It's difficult to grasp now, in an age when America is literally no more than a few hours away, but in the fifties a common form of transportation was still the horse and cart, just as it had been in biblical times. Milk and coal were delivered to our house by horse and cart. Bread was distributed from the bakers to the shops by horse and cart, and I still remember seeing the recently departed on their final journey in a horse-drawn hearse.

But on Sundays it was the church bells. The Blessed Sacrament Church summoned the faithful to mass at about seven o'clock and then again at about ten. Many of my friends were Catholic and they would frequently engage in arguments with other Catholics and the 'Proddy dogs'. With kids of the same faith they would argue about whether or not your soul had equal chances of salvation if you couldn't get out of bed for the seven o'clock mass and only managed the ten o'clock. With the Prods it was not so much an argument as an affirmation of fact. We were damned and that was all there was to it. Father O'Flynn or O'Malley or whoever had told them that all non-Catholics would suffer in the eternal fires of hell and they passed this gruesome message on to us.

'Listen, Al,' Peter Fannon said to me one day with an obviously genuine concern for my soul written all over his face. 'Honest to God, when you die you'll burn for ever in a great big fire if you don't become a Catholic. The priest said so and he doesn't tell lies.'

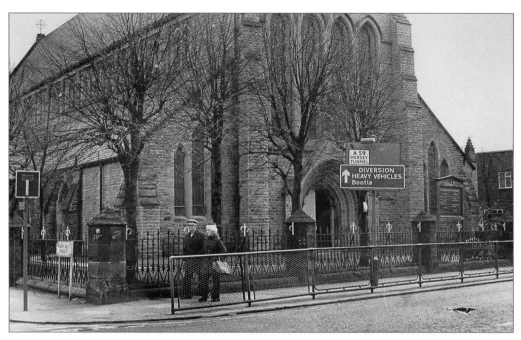

The Blessed Sacrament Church on Walton Vale. *(Liverpool Record Office)*

'Well, my dad says that's a load of rubbish,' I replied.

'No, it's not. It's gospel truth.'

'My dad says when you're dead you're dead. Only Catholics believe you burn in hell. And how do they know they're right? They can't prove it, can they?'

'Yes they can,' Peter answered.

'Go on, then,' I said, 'prove it.'

He proved it the only way he could. He punched me right on the end of my nose. There was a crunching sound inside my head, a flash of lightning behind my eyelids and then the blood squirted out, soaking my new jumper and staining it a dark, dirty crimson colour.

'There,' he said. 'God must have wanted me to bash you one for saying there's no hell or he'd have stopped me.'

Being less than ardent in my religious convictions, I had no wish to prolong this deep and meaningful theological debate. Some things were worth fighting and possibly dying for, like a toffee-apple or gob-stopper, but not religious dogma. Besides, Peter Fannon was bigger, heavier and niftier with his fists than I was, so I turned and ran off down the road. As I disappeared into the distance I could hear him shouting 'Yellow-bellied Proddie dog!'

He was right, of course. But it wasn't him I was scared of. I was afraid of what Mum was going to do when she saw the blood splattered all over my new jumper.

There was another sound that was absent on Sundays: the sound of kids playing out. Catholics, Protestants, Baptists, Methodists and all other -ists all had one thing

The Methodist church where the author attended Sunday School in the 1950s. *(Liverpool Record Office)*

in common. They all believed that God created the world in six days and rested on the seventh. So they all agreed that Sunday was to be a day of rest and that there was only one way to observe the Lord's day: don't allow the kids to do anything. The Ten Commandments were expanded to include: thou shalt not play in the street; thou shalt not go to the pictures; thou shalt not kick a ball around in the park; and, most arduous of all, the Commandment that we had to attend Sunday school.

I don't know why I was sent to Sunday school. The family was not religious and nobody else ever set foot in a church as far as I remember except for christenings, marriages and funerals. I don't even remember if my sister attended Sunday school. If she did, it was not at the Methodist church at the top of Cedar Road where I went. But then there is not much I remember about those Sunday afternoons of indescribable boredom, having to sit still for two hours listening to some weary woman trying to brainwash me into believing things I instinctively had considerable problems accepting as true. I could never understand why miracles only happened in the Holy Land two thousand years ago. I could never see what the problem was with God revealing himself to us. After all, if he just showed himself to us and told us exactly what he wanted us to do there would be no problem. It would stop all the arguments between Prods and Catholics and all the other different beliefs and then we could just get on with the important things in life like playing rally-o, nick-knock, or placing nails on the railway lines for the trains to run over. A six-inch carpentry nail, run over by a steam engine, would be converted into a perfectly flat, ten-inch long implement which, with just a little imagination, could become a gladiator's sword or Robin Hood's dagger. And that sort of insider knowledge was worth all the stories about turning water into wine or some shepherd who mislaid his sheep.

My downfall at Sunday school was Greek and Roman mythology. When Mr Lamden was talking to us in school about all the different gods and goddesses the Greeks and Romans had I would just sit entranced. There was something about the stories of Mars, Jupiter, Poseidon and all the rest that gripped me. They seemed to be more human and plausible than the saintly types we heard about in school assembly and Sunday school, and they certainly fired my imagination more. So when I asked why we were to understand that the Greek and Roman deities were only fictional, mythical characters but at the same time we were expected to believe that Jesus, Moses, Mary and Joseph were real people it did not go down very well. My argument was simple: the people of ancient Greece and Rome believed in their gods the way we were supposed to believe the stories in the Bible. How could we know we were right and they were wrong? As I say, this question was not received too well by our Sunday school teacher. Nor, I might add, did she answer it to my satisfaction.

But my Sunday school attendances came to a sudden and unexpected end. One day I came back carrying a red and gold certificate. Everyone in the class had been given one and asked ('ordered' would be closer to the truth) to sign it. I did so as well as my still primitive writing skills would allow me, although I had no idea what I was agreeing to.

'Do you know what this is, son?' Dad asked when I showed it to him.

'No.'

'It's the pledge.'

I was still none the wiser, and he explained.

'What you've done is sign a promise never to drink alcoholic drink.'

I did not understand what he meant by 'alcoholic drink'. When he explained that it meant that, when I grew up, I would not drink beer or whisky, I thought that this would perhaps be a good idea. At that age I did not even like the smell of his 'special lemonade', so I was not in the least perturbed at the thought of a life of abstinence.

'I'm not happy about this,' he said. 'They've no business getting you to sign things you don't understand.'

I never went again. My religious education would, in future, be confined to school assemblies and Mr Lamden's RE classes.

If the sound of Sunday was church bells, the smell of Sunday was cabbage. My mother had this idea that cabbage was only converted from its natural, crisp, crunchy state into a suitable vegetable for the Sunday dinner by boiling. But she boiled it for hours. She would start at about ten o'clock in the morning getting everything ready: peeling the spuds, cutting the carrots, getting the meat in the oven and getting the cabbage washed and cut into strips. Some weeks there would be a slight variation and it would be peas or sprouts, but this was very rare. Most of the time it was cabbage, cooked from ten o'clock in the morning until the dinner appeared on the table at three o'clock in the afternoon. By this time all the goodness in it would have been completely destroyed and what landed on the plate was almost indescribable. There would be a beautifully cooked roast, delicious roast and mashed potatoes, succulent carrots and . . . a soaking-wet, slimy mass of mushy, smelly cabbage. God knows why she made such a mess of cabbage, but she did. And she did so almost every Sunday. And the smell of boiling cabbage permeated the whole house so that there was nowhere, not a single room, not a single nook or cranny where you could escape it. Even Nan, sitting in the front room, bent almost double reading the *News of the World* with her magnifying glass, would occasionally pass some comment about the cabbage being almost ready now.

Why Mum took so long to prepare the meal was a mystery to many. During the week she had a very responsible job running an office for Bear Brand stockings in Liverpool. It was a job she held down for twenty-odd years so she must have been pretty efficient at it. But on Sundays her organisational skills just seemed to evaporate along with the water the cabbage was boiled in. Nobody could ever understand why, but I could. You don't have to be a skilled time and motion expert to realise that if you stop what you're doing every half hour for a cup of tea and a fag, then it slows things down considerably. But that was the way she worked and there was nothing anyone could do about it.

In summer, however, the normal schedule was occasionally subject to alteration. Sometimes, when the weather was fine, we would have a trip out to Southport, but what a planning nightmare that was! Christopher Columbus, Ferdinand Magellan and all the other explorers we were told about at school probably spent less time preparing to sail away on their voyages of discovery than Mum spent getting ready for a trip to Southport!

Liverpool is about fifteen miles from Southport, and in the days before universal car ownership the expedition had to be undertaken by bus. The big, shiny, red Ribble buses which served Lancashire outside the city boundaries ran every hour and the journey took about an hour and a half. Simple. For most people, dead easy. Get up in the morning, have a quick bite, put towels and swimming costumes in a little bag, close the door behind you and off you go. But not for us. Oh God no.

Nan and Granddad never came with us on these trips. Nor, as far as I can remember, did my sister. She was probably off out somewhere with her friends or boyfriend of the month, so it was just Mum, Dad and me. And that was enough. Mum insisted on making sandwiches, and if there had been any more than three of us going out for the day I dread to think how long it would have taken her to get ready. As it was, she would start making egg sandwiches, salmon paste sandwiches and all sorts of other kinds with flavours that escape me now. Then she would stop what she was doing and have a cup of tea and a fag. Now a few more sandwiches. Now another cup of tea and another fag. And all this while she was still in her dressing gown. She hadn't even started to get dressed yet.

It would by now be about eleven o'clock. I would have been ready for ages and so would be sitting about, bucket and spade at the ready, getting more and more impatient.

'Mum, when are we going?'

'Not long now, Al. Just got a few more sandwiches to make. Then I'll have a quick cuppa tea and we'll go.'

As soon as I heard those words I knew what she meant. The words 'quick' and 'cuppa tea' were almost a contradiction in terms for my mother. She couldn't have a cup of tea without a cigarette and a 'cuppa tea an' a fag' always meant sitting down and then she would start talking to anyone who was in hearing distance. She would go on and on about things that had happened in the office the previous week and would repeat verbatim conversations with anyone she'd had a disagreement with.

So she'd finish making the sandwiches, prepare a couple of flasks of tea, have another fag and then go upstairs to get ready. Dad, long dressed and ready, would open his paper and settle down for a good read and would almost certainly have time to make a reasonable stab at the crossword, if not finish it. And in the background *Two-way Family Favourites* would be playing records for servicemen stationed in Germany and Hong Kong. After an hour and a half of this came *The Billy Cotton Band Show*. In those days time could be measured in our house by radio programmes.

By the time we got out it would be about two o'clock in the afternoon. It was not uncommon for us to be driving into the bus station on Southport's Lord Street just before four o'clock, when most people were getting ready to pack up and go home.

7

Hogmanay & False Teeth

I am about seven years old. It's a cold winter's morning and it's still pitch dark when I open my eyes. Something at the end of the bed hypnotises me with fear. I can't move. All I can see, peering at me out of the darkness, is a glowing disk, hovering about five foot off the ground. It's like a face but it's got numbers around the edge and it seems to have two sticks, all shiny and green, which meet in the centre. I begin to wonder if Peter Fannon was right and if the devil has come to get me.

Then I remember. It's Christmas Day. I jump out of bed and switch the light on. There at the end of my bed, standing on top of my tallboy, is a beautiful pocket-watch with a luminous dial and its own little white plastic stand.

Dad often used to sing a song to me at bedtime about a little boy who had no daddy and was forgotten one year by Father Christmas. It was one of those tear-jerkers that ended up with the boy, whose requirements were very modest (a drum and some toy soldiers), having to go back and play with the previous year's broken toys on Christmas morning while his friends were opening their lovely new presents.

I used to cry my eyes out for that little lad, but I was not so sorry for him that I couldn't be happy when Santa remembered me. And he had remembered me this year. When I sat on his knee in Lewis's Grotto and asked him for a watch, I half expected him to forget. After all, he forgot the previous year, when I told him I wanted a real flint-lock pistol like the one Captain Blood had in the film I saw at the Walton Vale about pirates and walking the plank and Spanish galleons and cutlasses and hard-looking men with patches over their eyes. And he forgot the year before that, when I wanted a toy fire-engine like the one Ray Dowling had. Now all was forgiven and the watch more than made up for his previous amnesia, so I jumped on to Mum and Dad's bed to tell them the good news.

'Mum, Dad, look! Father Christmas 'as brought me a pocket watch! And it's got a chain, too!'

'Er, yeh, aawright, son,' said Dad, who was probably recovering from a skinful he'd had in the Sefton with Granddad the night before. 'Why don't you go and see what else you've got?'

I didn't know it at the time, but we had an unusual custom in our house. All my friends found their presents in socks or pillow cases at the end of their beds on Christmas morning. But I didn't. For some unknown reason my sister and I would

Lewis's department store, where the author visited Santa in his grotto. *(Sutton Collection)*

find our main present by our beds but then we had to go downstairs for the others. I say 'some unknown reason' but it was probably some crafty plan dreamt up by my mother to give her extra time in bed. She knew that if one of the presents downstairs was a book, like the *Dandy* or *Beano Annual*, I would spend a good couple of hours reading about Lord Snooty, Desperate Dan, Keyhole Kate and Corky the Cat. Quite a smart move, really.

But things didn't go quite according to plan that year. The watch was a wonderful present. But when I got downstairs I thought Lady Bountiful and Santa Claus had been particularly generous. In the sitting room, on one side of the cold, cheerless grate where yesterday's dead ashes languished, stood a pile of presents of various shapes and sizes, all neatly wrapped in gift paper. But protruding out of one parcel was a brown, imitation crocodile-leather strap.

'A holster!' I exclaimed. And I knew that nobody in this whole world would ever buy anyone just a holster, so there had to be a brand new, gleaming six-gun at the other end.

Faster than Roy Rogers could draw his gun I grabbed that parcel and tore off the wrapping paper. But there was no gun. Nor was there a holster. However, there was a beautiful handbag with special compartments for lipstick, a make-up compact and various other little pockets, some with zips and some without. When I looked at the label I understood my mistake: 'To Margaret, lots of love from Mum and Dad'.

My sister wasn't angry that I'd opened her present. She just treated the episode as another chance to comment on my unfailing genius for getting things wrong. I consoled myself with my watch, which was now in my dressing-gown pocket, as I curled up in Granddad's armchair with Desperate Dan getting stuck into some adventure before polishing off another whole cow pie, horns and all.

Christmas Day was a bit like a Sunday but with presents. Adults got up later than usual. Cooking smells permeated the house from mid-morning. A bottle of sherry appeared at about noon for the ladies in the house, Granddad would treat himself to a drachm of whisky and Dad would have a tot of rum.

But these differences were minor. The big difference was that the drawing room was brought into use. It felt so odd and yet pleasingly comfortable to be able to sit on the sheepskin rug in front of the fire in that room, playing with my new toys and then getting Dad to help me with this year's additional Meccano bits.

It was so warm and cosy in that room when there was a fire that one year I forgot myself and asked the question that nobody had ever dared ask. 'Why do we only use this room on Christmas Day?'

There was a deathly silence. All conversation stopped. The adults looked at each other, then at me, then at each other again. I felt as if I had asked for the secret of existence or for an explanation of the universe and all that's in it. It was my grand-mother who spoke:

'We have tae keep a best room fer the visitors. An' I'm no havin' the neighbours lookin' in on us frae ootside.'

And that was it in a nutshell. We were cramped together in the little 'front room' just so one room could be kept in pristine condition for the benefit of the neigh-bours. I never asked again.

Christmas was the highlight of the year for me. But for the family, being Scots, it was Hogmanay that was the real party. Christmas for the adults meant a few drinks, a few presents and turkey instead of a roast for dinner. But New Year's Eve was the big one and it was always referred to either as Hogmanay or Old Year's Night.

That tiny little house in Aintree was often full to overflowing on Old Year's Night. More often than not my mother's other brother, Uncle Jack, would come down from Edinburgh with Auntie Vi with all sorts of goodies I loved as a kid. There'd be Edinburgh rock, black bun loaf, clootie puddin' and shortbread, all things which were just not available in Liverpool.

At any time after about seven in the evening the party would begin. Uncle Jack, a talented musician, would get out his violin and start playing all the old favourites:

The author's Uncle Jack and Auntie Vi, part of the 'Edinburgh contingent' of the family, 1941. *(Author's collection)*

'She'll be comin' round the mountain'; 'Stop yer ticklin' Jock'; 'I love a lassie' and God knows how many more. After a few gins Mum and Auntie Vi would do a rendition of 'South of the border, Down Mexico way' and 'I'll take you home again Kathleen'. A bit later Nan would insist on doing the Highland Fling, and then we'd all have a bash at the Gay Gordons and Granddad would show his more sentimental side, reminiscing tearfully about his childhood and youth north of the border.

Then came the climax of the evening. At about eleven o'clock Nan would start worrying about who was going to be the 'first foot'. This was a noble and ancient custom she and Granddad had brought with them when they moved down from Scotland, to the amusement of all our Scouse neighbours. It involved selecting a member of the family or a very close friend to be the first person across the threshold after the stroke of midnight. And a crucial part of his duties was to carry a lump of coal and a quarter pound of tea as symbols of good luck and those commodities that were the basic essentials for life: food and warmth. It's a custom associated with the greeting 'lang may yer lum reek' ('may your chimney always smoke').

Just before midnight everyone would go outside, even on the coldest of nights, to listen to the hooters on the ships in the Mersey sounding the start of the new year. The elected person would perform his 'first-foot' duties. Then it was 'Auld Lang Syne', another wee tot or drachm, and that was it. Like melting snow the celebrations gradually began to fade away as the various partygoers' stamina ran out and they all eventually had had enough and decided it was time for bed. I seem to remember that Uncle Jack and Mum kept going the longest.

The only time I ever saw Granddad without his false teeth in was New Year's Day 1955. I remember it distinctly. The previous evening he had been particularly enthusiastic with his support for the Johnnie Walker distillery and was now feeling rather fragile. As I was getting dressed I could hear him saying uncomplimentary things about Dad who, by this time, was already out at work. As I listened it became obvious that he had somehow become fixated with the idea that Dad had gone to work with his (Granddad's) false teeth. Why Dad would want to borrow somebody else's false teeth I can't imagine as he had a perfectly good set of dentures of his own. But there was no convincing Granddad. He couldn't find his teeth so there was only one explanation. Dad had taken them, either by mistake or design, but he had definitely taken them.

Granddad couldn't eat his breakfast. He had nothing to chew with. He normally ate eggs and slightly cooked, almost raw bacon, but without his teeth he couldn't even think about it. Nor could he enjoy a decent lunch, and consequently he was in a foul mood all day. He kept looking at the clock, muttering, 'Where the hell's Bob wi' ma teeth? It's New Year's Day, surely he's no workin' all day t'day?'

'I haven't got your teeth', Dad protested when he came home and was immediately challenged on the matter of the aforesaid dentures. 'I've got my own. What do I want yours for?'

The altercation continued for some time until Dad (ever the voice of reason!) decided to do something more constructive than get involved in an argument over something that probably had a very simple explanation. He looked for the dentures in the bathroom, under Nan and Granddad's bed, under their dressing table. Nothing. Couldn't find them anywhere. Then he had a brainwave. He turned his attention once more to their bed and pulled back the eiderdown. There they were. Crisis over. Granddad could eat again.

The incident was never referred to in our house again. Well, not for a couple of hours anyway. Then poor old Granddad never lived it down.

8

Reluctantly to School

In September 1953 I moved up into Miss Fish's class. Either by accident or design it fell to her lot to prepare her charges for the Eleven Plus exam. Although we did not actually sit the exam until we had moved up into Mr Lamden's class, her task was to give us a year of solid swotting in arithmetic and English. Presumably the thinking was that after a year of Miss Fish's no-nonsense approach to the acquisition of learning Mr Lamden would only need to add the finishing touches and fill in the gaps in our knowledge in time for the examination which we would all pass with flying colours. At least, that was the theory.

Now Miss Fish had a fearsome reputation in Rice Lane Junior School. For most of the previous year we all looked forward with trepidation to the day when she would take over as our mentor in matters academical. And she was every bit as stern as the reputation that preceded her. She stood no messing and she could wield the cane as viciously and enthusiastically as any of her male colleagues.

But there was another reason Miss Fish was well known outside the boundaries of her own class. Indeed she was well known beyond the limits of the school for a certain eccentricity which, in those days, set her apart from other members of her sex but today nobody would even bat an eyelid at: she dressed like a man. The only sop she made to the Cerberus of contemporary convention was that, in school at least, she always wore a skirt. But it was always the same style. In the three or four years I spent at that school I never saw her in anything else. It was always the same. Men's heavy brown brogue shoes, thick woollen stockings, a heavy grey, herringbone-pattern skirt and matching jacket. Under her jacket she always wore a man's shirt with detachable collar, and a tie. And to crown it all she had her hair cut just like a man's. Short back and sides with a right parting and held in place with Brylcreem.

But I have to say she could recognise talent when she spotted it. On my very first morning in her class she appointed me as ink monitor. She must have realised that out of the whole class I was the only one with shoulders broad enough to take on the onerous responsibilities concomitant with the position. I had to be in school at least fifteen minutes before everybody else in the morning so that I could make up the day's supply of ink for the class. This involved taking about a quarter of a pound of ink powder and mixing it with a couple of pints of water and stirring until all the powder had dissolved. If you didn't stir the mixture long enough, the powder would not dissolve properly and the result would be a gooey mess that clogged up the steel pens we all had to write with in those days.

When the ink had been correctly prepared I then had to walk around the classroom and pour the ink from a jug into each individual ink-well in every desk. If I hadn't finished by the time Miss Fish appeared she would want to know the reason why.

Now I always felt that as I carried out my duties as ink monitor with such unstinting enthusiasm and unfailing efficiency I should have been allowed a certain leeway when it came to my own lack of proficiency in manipulating the steel-nibbed, dip-in pen. But Miss Fish and I disagreed on this point. She showed me no particular favours. If I blotted my copybook, literally rather than metaphorically, she would make me hold out my hand and give me a thwack with her cane that left me unable to even hold a pen, let alone write, for at least a quarter of an hour.

Then there were Friday mornings. Every Friday before morning playtime Miss Fish gave us all an arithmetic test consisting of thirty sums. Those of us who got twenty-five or more correct were allowed to go to the school film show in the assembly hall after playtime. Those who did not reach this score got one stroke of the cane on each hand and had to do the test again while everyone else was watching films. I got to the film show no more than about three times in the whole year.

The fact that the films shown were all educational (i.e. boring as hell) was beside the point. It was a humiliating experience to be one of only half a dozen kids in the whole school, week in, week out, to be forced to redo a test while everybody else was enjoying a break from English and arithmetic lessons. Not that the films were all that good. Of the few I did see that year I remember one about the wonders of 'Wheat farming in the Canadian Prairies', another about 'Plant life along the river Wye' and then a mind-numbing, excruciatingly tedious film about how vegetables get put into tins in factories. If the Walton Vale had shown these at a 'kids' crush' there would have been a riot. No self-respecting cinema manager would have risked his reputation (or possibly his life!) by showing such unpalatable drivel.

But Friday mornings in many respects summed up the educational policies, not just of Miss Fish or even Rice Lane Junior School, but of the whole educational establishment. My experience was no different from that of most children who attended school before the enlightened sixties or seventies and basically the approach was humiliation and/or the cane.

I often wonder if the proponents of such methods ever realised the anguish and psychological torture children went through in those bleak days. I, and I'm sure I wasn't the only one, used to go to bed terrified on Thursday night, dreading the following morning and hoping it would never dawn.

But it wasn't just the kids who worried. Parents also had many sleepless nights and anxious hours worrying over whether or not their offspring would pass the scholarship. And it wasn't only a question of academic prowess; it was also a question of social standing. Somehow having a son or daughter at a grammar school gave working-class mums and dads some sort of kudos which they didn't enjoy if Jack or Jill went to the secondary modern. It was as if the parents could bathe in the reflected glory of their intellectually superior sons and daughters.

So no effort was spared. All the stops were pulled out and most parents took advantage of any additional help that could be mustered in their quest for the Holy

Grail of a place at the grammar school for their children. And my parents were no exception, although I have to admit that it was mainly my mother who was the instigator of various stratagems to increase my chances of success.

I knew I had reason to be worried when I spotted Mum in deep conversation with Miss Fish one day outside Maudaunts the fishmongers. I couldn't hear a word they were saying, but I could tell from the look on their faces that they were discussing something serious and not just passing the time of day. Mum didn't gossip. Unlike many of the women in the neighbourhood she did not stand for hours with someone she had chanced upon while out shopping and talk endlessly about who was doing what with whom. No, that was not the kind of thing she did. So when she seemed to spend an inordinately long time talking to Miss Fish my paranoia clicked into gear and my tiny mind started coming up with all sorts of possible explanations. Was I in some kind of trouble at school I didn't yet know about? Had I been late for ink-monitor duties? Had June Carter snitched on me for pulling her pig-tails? Or was Miss Fish telling Mum about catching me having a wee behind the air-raid shelters?

I had no idea. I just couldn't imagine what was afoot but I didn't have to wait long to find out. It was like a bombshell and it exploded in our kitchen just as Mum was clearing away the tea dishes.

'By the way,' she said, lighting her post-prandial fag, 'I've been talking to your teacher and we both think you could do with some extra tuition. Starting tomorrow you're having private lessons at her house for an hour and half after school on Thursdays.'

That was one explanation for their tête-à-tête that had never occurred to me. Had it been a caning offence I could have coped with it. I'd been caned on my left hand, caned on my right hand and caned on my bottom so many times that another 'six of the best' would have been easy-peasy. Less acceptable, but still endurable, would have been staying in after school for half an hour to do a hundred lines. But private tuition? Did Mum really hate me that much? Wasn't it unspeakable torture enough just having to be in school five days a week from nine until four without having another hour and a half tacked on to the end of every week? I was stunned into abject silence and I started to feel sick. I was in a desperate situation and desperate situations demand desperate measures. After all, I had enough on my mind on Thursday nights worrying about the test on Friday without having another load of torture heaped on me. I had to think of something.

Now any kid will tell you that when all else fails there's always illness. Parents do not like the thought of their little ones being ill. They always buckle if they think there is the slightest danger that their little dears might have caught something serious. And in those days 'serious' meant the scourge of the land, polio. Several kids in school had had it and they had to wear leg braces and probably would have to for the rest of their lives. 'Nature's cruel architect', one wit called it, because of the way it could twist and deform young limbs.

I'm ashamed now to think of the way I played on my parents' fears without so much as a twinge of conscience. But at the time I was doing no more than using an effective subterfuge in my constant battle with grown-ups. They could do whatever they wanted to make me do things their way, so what was wrong with my doing whatever I wanted to avoid doing things their way?

The next morning, then, when I should have been getting dressed to go to school I went into action. With a virtuoso performance any matinée idol would have been proud of I came downstairs and told Mum and Dad I wasn't feeling well.

'What's wrong?' Mum asked

'Got a headache and tummy ache. . . .'

'Oh, you'll be all right. You probably just need some opening medicine.'

That was always Mum's first line of defence against any affliction in the family. And, as usual, her first suggestion was a healthy dose of Andrew's Liver Salts, and if they didn't have the desired effect it would be a couple of tablespoons of syrup of figs.

Things were not going well. Things were not going according to plan. It was time for a further turn of the screw.

'. . . and I've got this funny feeling in my legs.'

That was it. That did the trick. She looked at me in horror and told me to get back to bed right away and to stay there. Then she turned to Granddad and asked him if he could go and phone for the doctor and stay in until he came.

Of course Dr Bannerman could find nothing wrong with me. But by the time he arrived and made his diagnosis it was far too late for me to get dressed and go to school. So I just kept my dressing gown on and played with my Meccano all afternoon. Then I started a game of snakes and ladders with Granddad. I was doing quite well and had zoomed ahead up several long ladders when my luck suddenly changed, in more ways than one. My counter had just landed on one of the longest snakes on the board and was about to suffer a steep descent when Mum came in. She took one look at me and realised that my 'illness' was a total sham. By subterfuge I had missed school and Miss Fish's private lesson, made her late for work and probably got her into further trouble with her boss as she had also left early because she was worried about me. I had just slid down one snake but now I was precipitated up the 'ladder' in our hall and back to bed. And going to bed at five o'clock in the afternoon when there's nothing wrong with you is no joke.

The next morning I got dressed as usual to go off to school. As I was coming down the stairs Mum was standing at the bottom, obviously waiting for me.

'Where are you going?' she asked.

'I'm going to school.'

'Oh no you're not. You were very ill yesterday so you can't possibly be better yet. Now get back up those stairs and get undressed and into bed.'

I couldn't believe my luck. She must have thought I was ill after all! And I was going to miss the arithmetic test!

But I was a little too quick with my silent rejoicing. The regime she prescribed for me was a lesson I never forgot. She managed somehow to get a day off work so that she could make sure none of her prison regulations were abused, forgotten or broken.

At lunchtime she made me get out of bed, get dressed and go downstairs to eat. There was going to be no such thing as meals in bed for the little invalid. Oh no. Then, as soon as I had finished eating I had to go back upstairs and get undressed again and into bed. When it was teatime I had to get out of bed again, get dressed, go downstairs, have my meal, go back upstairs, get undressed and into bed again. And it was exactly the same on Saturday. And again on Sunday. By Sunday evening I had had enough. I couldn't stand the sight of my bedroom any more. My apologies were accepted. It was a very hard lesson, but it worked. Never again did I try to avoid anything by feigning illness.

And the experience had a strange effect on my attitude to school. By comparison with staying in bed all weekend, when I could hear my friends shouting and laughing as they played out in the street, school was transformed into a place of wonder and delight. The Friday test miraculously lost its terror for me and Miss Fish, overnight, ceased to be a source of terror and foreboding. In fact, all of a sudden I started looking forward to going to school and, believe it or not, I even began to enjoy some of the lessons.

But this belated love affair with education did little good. My sudden enthusiasm for writing essays in conjunction with my lessening antipathy towards arithmetic arrived too late to be of any help to me on the Day of Judgement. The sun rose on the day of the scholarship examination. The sun set on the day of the scholarship examination. And in between these two cosmic events I travelled into town, to the Liverpool Institute, and sat the Eleven Plus.

But I failed.

9

Aintree Nights

Entertainment in those days was of a very different hue. Radio was well established, television was just beginning to make its mark, but the cinema reigned supreme. Just around the corner from Grace Road we had the Walton Vale picture-house and half a mile further on was the Palace, next door to Aintree Bowls Club. In the other direction, up Moss Lane, was the Carlton and all three establishments thrived. Most nights of the week there would be a reasonable attendance at these temples to entertainment, but on Fridays and Saturdays they were packed.

But there was an alternative form of entertainment: the church social. Now just a fading memory in the minds of old duffers rapidly approaching senility, these gatherings were a wonderful form of family entertainment. In an age of discos, flashing lights, strident music and alcohol-fuelled exhibitionism it is difficult to believe that, only a couple of generations ago, the Church played an active role in

The Carlton cinema was built in the 1930s. It was one of the most popular in the area and was packed most nights of the week in the 1950s and early '60s. (*Liverpool Record Office*)

providing entertainment for the whole community, young and old, and that the generations actually came together and mixed. This was Saturday night fun before the invention of the generation gap.

Sometimes these 'socials' would take the form of amateur variety shows. I well remember going to the Methodist church hall with Mum and Dad to watch what can only be described as good old-fashioned entertainment. And the minister or the local scoutmaster (the 7th Aintree pack) would introduce the acts. Someone would tell a funny story (never smutty!). Someone else would do a little song-and-dance routine and then someone else might come on and either read or recite a passage from Dickens. But I always looked forward to the old man who occasionally came on the stage and recited those wonderful Victorian monologues such as George Sims's 'It was Christmas Day in the Workhouse' or Robert Service's 'The Shooting of Dan McGrew' and 'The Ballad of Blasphemous Bill'.

One night there was a brand new form of musical interlude. Cyril Bailey, one of the scout leaders, walked on to the stage and announced that he had managed to acquire, for one performance only and at virtually no expense, the not exactly famous and certainly not world-renowned (nobody had probably heard of them outside Aintree) 'Pete Something-or-other Skiffle group'.

In these days of all manner of electronic, all-singing, all-dancing synthesisers, mixers and God knows what other kinds of so-called 'musical instruments' the 'skiffle' group seems positively antediluvian. The typical group would consist of four lads in drainpipe trousers, crew-neck sweaters and their hair brushed up into as tall a quiff as they could manage. Their instruments were basic in the extreme. In fact, the only real instrument was the guitar or guitars; the rest were improvised. There would be a contraption that produced sounds similar to those from a double bass but which bore scarcely any resemblance to the real thing in shape or form. The sensuous curves and beautiful craftsmanship were no longer to be seen and the skiffle version was made of an old tea-chest, a piece of string and a brush-handle. Then there was the washboard. A real, genuine washboard such as the old women used not so many years earlier for scrubbing a family's clothes in the days before washing machines and even washing powder. And the deluxe version of this highly prized skiffle instrument had a bell or old car hooter attached for additional effect.

Such primitive improvisation sounds as if any attempt to produce what might just about pass for music would be doomed to humiliating failure from the word go. But it worked. It actually worked. When three or four lads with reasonable ability put it all together, the sounds they could produce with such basic equipment could actually be considered entertainment and could set even the most geriatric, arthritic feet a-tappin'.

On other nights the church social took the form of a dance. And it didn't matter if these dances were held at the Methodist church or at St John's near Rice Lane School, the format was always the same. But to understand what they were like anybody born later than about 1960 has to clear his or her mind completely of modern notions of what dancing as a form of social entertainment should be like. There were no flashing lights, no DJs with an inexhaustible supply of thumping,

The 7th Aintree Cub Pack. Cyril Bailey is standing on the right at the back. The author is third from the left, kneeling, second row from the front. *(Author's collection)*

drumming, tuneless, ear-splittingly-loud cacophonous music. You did not stand a million miles away from the person you were supposed to be dancing with and gyrate in a display of narcissistic exhibitionism. Oh no. Things were far more sedate.

For a start the music would be provided by a lady of a certain age (disparagingly referred to by a friend of mine as 'Miss Neveradit') giving a virtuoso performance on the piano, a moustachioed, chain-smoking gentleman on a set of drums who made great use of what looked to me like a wire brush, and someone else playing a guitar. And they would play waltzes, quicksteps, foxtrots and all the other dances out of the ballroom repertoire. But (and it's a big 'but') the main difference between then and now was that you could get hold of the girl you were dancing with and could talk to her.

Now these dances usually started at about seven o'clock. And they almost always followed a strict pattern. The girls in their wide, hooped dresses and sparkly shoes would all stand at one side of the room. The boys in their 'drainies' would be at the other side. The girls would look at the boys and the boys would look at the girls, so that this part of the evening looked more like a confrontation than a prelude to a kiss later on behind the bus-shelter.

At about eight o'clock, to get things moving, the MC (master of ceremonies) would organise a Paul Jones to break the ice a bit. This involved two concentric circles (girls in the inner one, boys in the outer) moving in different directions while the band played some jaunty tune. When the music stopped you took hold of the hand of the girl facing you, and when the music started up, off you both went dancing round the room. Excellent. No problem. All the embarrassment of walking across the floor to ask someone for a dance had gone.

At some stage in the proceedings the vicar or scout leader or whoever was doing a stint that week as the MC would announce that the band deserved a break and we would all clap politely. Then he would go over to an ancient, wind-up gramophone, sort out some vinyl 78s and the 'barn dance' time of the evening would begin. Young and old, we would all take our partners for the Virginia Reel, the Valeta, the Saint Bernard's Waltz, the Gay Gordons and the Barn Dance. Yes, we did. In a working class district of Liverpool a mere couple of generations ago!

But the entertainment did not stop there. There was always an interval when the fun didn't stop, it just changed character. Now it was competition time. Mr Carr, one of the scout leaders and a very dapper gentleman with slicked-back, Brylcreemed hair, used to take charge of this. He would organise competitions to see which of the ladies present had made the most delicious Victoria sponge cake, the best treacle toffee or the most succulent apple pie. And he revelled in it. He charmed the ladies and, I remember, made those who were disappointed or who hadn't done so well feel as if they would be winners next time.

But he did come seriously unstuck, poor man, on one occasion. About an hour or so before the start of the dance all the ladies would bring their goodies for tasting by a 'panel of experts'. On this particular occasion all the ladies came along with their treacle toffee neatly cut into squares and deposited in little paper bags, just like the ones used in a real sweetshop. The bags were placed along the table near the entrance and then the experts did their job. Mr Carr then consulted with them and between them they decided on a winner.

At the appropriate time during the interval Mr Carr stood up and made pleasing remarks about how high the standard was and how difficult it was to make a choice.

'But there has to be a winner,' he pronounced, 'and this week the winner is Mrs Thompson. Her toffee was a delight to eat. Not too sweet and just the right balance between brittleness and softness.'

Everyone clapped. Then Mr Carr spoke again.

'Of course there also has to be a loser, who will receive the wooden spoon, and we hope she will take it in good grace and not be deterred from having another go next time. But the panel just felt that her toffee was a touch too sweet and a little too brittle.' He then presented the wooden spoon to another lady in the room.

There was more applause, although this time more as a sign of encouragement than congratulation.

Mr Carr was just about to announce that the band was now fully refreshed and ready to treat us to another hour or so of waltzes and quicksteps, when Mr Thompson, the winner's husband, stood up.

'Excuse me,' he said, 'I just have a few words to add. I was very pleased at your kind words about my wife's toffee and I would like to offer my sympathies to the loser. But you might like to know that both sets of toffee were the same.'

It turned out that Mr Thompson had, for a practical joke, removed all little bags of toffee from the table and replaced them with bags of toffee all made by his wife! The winner and loser were exactly the same.

Mr Carr blushed and laughed to hide his embarrassment. What Mr Carr said to Mr Thompson when everyone had gone home history does not record.

10

Target Practice

On a beautiful, sunny morning in September 1955 I closed the front door behind me, walked to the top of Grace Road and turned right. No more than fifteen minutes later I had walked past the Walton Vale cinema, crossed Cedar Road, passed the Black Bull and was at my destination: Warbreck Secondary Modern School. This was to be the seat of learning which would have an incalculable influence on the rest of my life and where, for the next two years, I would learn valuable lessons both in and out of the classroom.

In those days the educational system in Liverpool (as in most of the rest of the country) was rigidly divisive. Children who did well in the Eleven Plus examination and were considered suitable material for an academic education went to a grammar school. Those who did not do quite so well were offered places in a commercial

Warbreck Secondary Modern School. This building, dating from 1896, was demolished in the late 1990s to make way for a more modern one. *(Liverpool Record Office)*

school, and those who seemed to have an aptitude for technical subjects went to a technical school. Those who fitted into none of the above categories were thought of in the non-politically correct terminology of the times as dunces and were considered virtually incapable of grasping anything beyond the very basics of education. These were deemed to be the future Orwellian proles – the manual labourers and drudges of a society which was becoming more and more of a meritocracy.

The wrought-iron gates of that Victorian Moloch, then, opened on that September morn at about 8.45 and prepared to swallow a hundred or so new boys before crunching them, grinding them and spitting them out a few years later to be society's labourers and sweated-brow toilers. Like zombies we walked through the gates and into what seemed to me to be an enormous expanse of the playground where we were told to stand in lines, according to whichever junior school we had been at the previous year. And there we stood, basking in the rays of the late summer sun, waiting to be told what to do next.

And we did not have to wait long. Fairly soon a rather slightly built teacher (whom I did not know then but later was to know as Mr Bent) appeared as if from nowhere and divided us up into groups, ready to be led away by older boys to our respective new classrooms. I ended up with Mr Brewer (known affectionately as 'Danny', but I never did find out if it was his real name), who for the next year had the not too enviable task of trying to educate us. All in all he did a reasonable job, but he did seem to have some fixation with the Babylonians and set us the same ten questions on their history for a test about once a month for the whole year.

But the most fascinating thing about our new classroom on that first day had nothing to do with the excitement of the new world of academe that was about to open before me. Nor was it the few battered textbooks which were handed out to us (some of them dating back to the 1920s) or the fact that the lad sitting next to me could not read even the simplest words like 'the' and 'school'. In fact his embarrassingly incompetent attempts to read aloud brought giggles and sniggers from his new classmates and this made matters even worse for him. Not surprisingly, he turned against school and found solace dreaming about the motorbike he was going to buy as soon as he was old enough to get his licence. Unfortunately, only a couple of years later the poor lad was killed when he crashed his newly acquired motorbike into a wall by the Black Bull pub.

No. The most fascinating thing about that classroom were the ink-bombs stuck to the ceiling. Thousands of them. Previous generations of that august establishment had obviously taken the study of ballistics very seriously and devoted many hours to gunnery practice to see who could stick the most ink-bombs on the ceiling.

In those days when a biro was still a rarity, ink-wells and blotting paper provided wonderful ammunition for snotty-nosed kids who nurtured within their bosoms a latent interest in the mechanics and mathematics associated with the study of projectiles. After all, getting your ink-bomb to stick to the ceiling was not just a matter of flicking it in the air and hoping for the best. On the contrary, there were several variables to take into account every time a shot was fired. You had to try to work out the optimum weight of the projectile if success was to be guaranteed. This meant a calculation of how much blotting paper had to be torn off the sheet, how long it should be steeped in the ink and then whether or not a steel or wooden ruler made the better launch-pad. Then there was the question of the trajectory. If its intended target was the ceiling it was placed on the end of a ruler and projected perpendicularly upwards. If the ruler had been bent just enough to produce the correct muzzle velocity and the weight and degree of ink saturation were just right, there was a good chance that the bomb would stick to the ceiling and remain there for days, weeks or even years. Some of the boys claimed they could identify bombs left by their fathers a whole generation earlier.

But the ceiling was not the only target. When Mr Brewer was standing with his back towards us as he wrote on the blackboard, war would break out. The boys on one side of the classroom would suddenly decide that an artillery bombardment of those on the other side was in order. Then additional calculations and advanced mathematics came into the picture. Not only were the correct size and weight of the projectile to be calculated but also the trajectory. Targets closer to the aggressor required a higher parabola; targets further away demanded a parabola which stayed lower but covered more ground for the energy released by the ruler.

The result of all this was positively surreal. Mr Brewer was busy writing out sums on the blackboard which really any self-respecting primary school kid should have been able to tackle with little difficulty. Behind him a war was being waged involving calculations and a knowledge and understanding of ballistics and higher mathematics which we just seemed to acquire naturally and without any textbooks. There must be a lesson for educationalists in there somewhere!

There was something of the Victorian about 'Danny' Brewer, both literally and figuratively. He was probably in his early sixties, which would mean that when he was born Victoria was still on the throne. And he seemed to have retained many of the attitudes and concepts of world history prevalent at the turn of the century. He would sit at the front of the class at a high Dickensian desk and when we had to have work marked we would all have to walk to the front and stand in a line by it. From his high vantage point he would peer down at us through his horn-rimmed spectacles as he tut-tutted and highlighted our mistakes with a red pencil.

He was also, as many of his generation, a bit of an imperialist. His history lessons often involved the story of how the British Empire came into being, and he could scarcely contain his patriotic jingoism (or should that be jingoistic patriotism?) as he told us how we should all get down on our knees and thank God that we had been born British. At the time I didn't argue as he was only repeating ideas and attitudes which the vast majority of the population held anyway. Now I cringe, but in those days nobody questioned the basic belief that Englishmen had a God-given right to travel around the globe imposing their culture, customs and language on other nations whether they wanted them or not.

It was in Mr Brewer's class that most of us began to be aware of the wider world. Events were hotting up on the international scene, and at home and in school conversations reflected the serious situation the country was in and the possibility not just of war but of nuclear war. The Egyptian president, Gamal Abdel Nasser, nationalised the Suez Canal, so France and Britain (to the fury of the Americans) sent in the army to retake it by force. And in Europe Soviet Russia sent the tanks into Budapest to crush the Hungarian uprising. By any standards things were looking pretty bleak, but Mr Brewer's sangfroid was unshakeable. 'Don't worry,' he said when we asked him if we were all going to be killed in a nuclear war. 'We're British and the British might lose the odd battle but they always win the war.' Such faith allowed me to sleep at night.

If Mr Brewer retained something of the Victorian schoolmaster, the headmaster Mr Taylor (universally known as Fred but this time it was his real name) was the very embodiment of one. His office was immediately opposite the main entrance to the school building and every morning from about 8.45 he would stand there in his academic gown, gold pocket-watch in hand, and survey us as we filed past on the way to our classrooms. On winter mornings the Dickensian picture was complete: imagine a short, slightly portly man in an academic gown with a gold watch-chain straddling his tummy standing in front of the open door of his office, and a roaring fire in a Victorian grate just visible behind him. Such was the picture that greeted us on frosty mornings. Such was the picture that did not differ all that much from the image of Wackford Squeers of Dotheboys Hall in the ancient edition of *Nicholas Nickleby* in the class library.

Two teachers at Warbreck Secondary Modern School had an incalculable effect on my life. In fact, it is no exaggeration to say that had I gone to that school a year earlier or a year later the whole course of my life would probably been very different. The reason for this can be summed up in one word: French.

The belated interest in school subjects which I began to experience in my final days at Rice Lane was really no more than the merest stirring which, despite its welcome presence, did not actually blossom into what might be described as a full-blown passion for anything even vaguely intellectual. But then everything changed in a quite dramatic fashion.

On one of the first days at my new school Mr Brewer walked out of the classroom and in came Mr (or Monsieur, as we all soon called him) Matheson. Slim, tallish, with black hair and a beautiful thick red beard, this was the man who was to introduce me to languages and set me on the path of my future career.

'*Bonjour, la classe*,' he said, and I was transfixed. It was as sudden as that. There was something at once magical and musical about the way he pronounced these foreign words that sealed my future. It wasn't a decision I arrived at after due thought and consideration. It was more of a feeling I had inside that I wanted to find out as much as possible about this wonderful new sound called French. There was just something beautiful, even sensuous, about hearing and then imitating all those strange nasal sounds and the seductive intonation that captivated me. I found myself actually looking forward to the half hour or so each day that was devoted to French, and as soon as I heard those words '*Bonjour, la classe*,' the adrenalin started to flow and I wanted Monsieur Matheson to get as much French into me as thirty-five minutes would allow.

'Class of 55' at Warbreck. The headmaster, Mr Taylor, is seated centre front. Mr 'Danny' Brewer is standing on the left; the author is standing sixth from the left on the back row. The teacher on the far right is Mr Corrin. (*Author's collection*)

At night I read the French textbook in bed. The only problem was that I did not have the necessary background in grammar to understand everything the book was talking about. I knew what nouns, verbs and adverbs were, as Miss Fish had given us a good grounding in them. But I was a bit flummoxed when I found out that in French adjectives usually came after the noun and that if a noun was in the plural the adjective had to be as well. But the real killer was gender. Finding out that all nouns (table, chair, dog as well as the obvious ones like girl or boy) had to be either masculine or feminine was a bit of a surprise.

I drove Mum and Dad mad asking them questions they couldn't possibly answer as neither of them had any idea about foreign languages. But I just couldn't wait. If I read something I couldn't understand I would put my dressing-gown on and make my way downstairs to ask them. Mum just said she hadn't got a clue but poor Dad would at least take hold of the book and try to answer my question. When I recall those occasions now I cannot help thinking that he must have suffered acute embarrassment. Only a few months earlier they had almost given up on my ever being able to cope with even the most rudimentary educational instruction, and now here I was asking them questions they hadn't got a snowball's chance in hell of answering. So the usual outcome was for Dad to admit defeat and just say, quietly, 'Sorry, son, you'll have to ask Mr Matheson in the morning.'

11

The Spy Within

Stalin died in 1953. I remember his face on the front of the *News Chronicle* with some funny Russian writing underneath. In 1956 the Russians crushed the uprising in Hungary. Newspaper reports of the fighting often showed funny Russian writing underneath.

One frosty morning, also in 1956, Dad asked me to go over the road to Gribby's the newsagents and get him ten Woodbines. As I came out of the shop my eye was attracted to the little envelopes of foreign stamps stuck in the window. Some had faces on with funny Russian writing underneath.

'Dad,' I said when I got back home with his 'Woodies', 'why don't the Russians have the same writing as us?'

'Dunno, son,' said Dad, lighting his cigarette and trying to pick a horse in the 3.30 at Doncaster or York or wherever. 'Better ask your teachers. They should know.' That was the end of the conversation, but it was not the end of the matter. My curiosity had been aroused and I decided I was going to find out. I was now obsessed with the idea of learning the Russian alphabet but I had no idea how to go about it. The local library had books on Spanish, French and German, but nothing on Russian. None of the teachers at Warbreck could help me and if I asked any of my friends I was met with a mixture of suspicion and incredulity. They could not believe any normal person could be bothered to find out about the Russian alphabet. The only possible explanation as far as they were concerned was that I was at least a potential if not already an active spy.

Then Fate came to my help in the strangest of ways.

Our next-door neighbour, Arthur Hart, was a widower who had been in the Liverpool police since the 1920s and was just coming up to retirement. One dark November night he came home off duty and, as he was putting his key in the lock, he just happened to look down and saw water pouring out from under the door. When he opened it what greeted him almost reduced the poor man to tears. The tank in the loft had burst and water had been pouring, probably for hours, down through the ceilings and cascading down the stairs. He stepped into the pitch-dark hall and immediately felt his feet sink into the sodden carpet and, as he put his hand out to switch on the light, he could feel the water landing on his head and hands as it poured through the hall ceiling. Fortunately he realised what must have happened and decided that the best thing to do was not to touch anything electrical and to leave things until the next morning.

Аа $\mathcal{A}$ a	Кк $\mathcal{K}$ $\varkappa$	Хх $\mathcal{X}$ x
Бб $\mathcal{B}$ δ	Лл $\mathcal{L}$ $\varkappa$	Цц $\mathcal{U}$ $\varkappa$
Вв $\mathcal{B}$ θ	Мм $\mathcal{M}$ $\varkappa$	Чч $\mathcal{U}$ $\varkappa$
Гг $\mathcal{T}$ ι	Нн $\mathcal{H}$ $\varkappa$	Шш $\mathcal{U}$ $\varkappa$
Дд $\mathcal{D}$ g ∂	Оо $\mathcal{O}$ o	Щщ $\mathcal{U}$ $\varkappa$
Ее $\mathcal{E}$ e	Пп $\mathcal{T}$ n	Ыы $\mathcal{U}$ $\varkappa$
Ёё $\mathcal{E}$ $\ddot{e}$	Рр $\mathcal{P}$ p	Ъъ $\mathcal{Z}$ $\varkappa$
Жж $\mathcal{Ж}$ $\varkappa$	Сс $\mathcal{C}$ c	Ьь $\mathcal{Z}$ ι
Зз $\mathcal{Z}$ z	Тт $\mathcal{Tm}$ τ	Ээ $\mathcal{Э}$ z
Ии $\mathcal{U}$ u	Уу $\mathcal{У}$ y	Юю $\mathcal{Ю}$ $\varkappa$
Йй $\mathcal{U}$ $\breve{u}$	Фф $\mathcal{Ф}$ φ	Яя $\mathcal{Я}$ $\varkappa$

The Russian alphabet, which so fascinated the author as a boy.

So he came next door to our house. Mum took him inside and made him a cup of tea. Dad (who always knew what to do in emergencies) went round and managed somehow to turn the water off at the mains.

After several cups of tea, a few hastily rustled-up slices of cheese on toast and a huge wedge of Mum's home-made apple pie, Arthur said he would go round to his daughter's for the night and come back the next morning to start sorting out the mess. When he did appear the next day we all traipsed round to see what state his house was in. To cut a long story short the place was uninhabitable. All the carpets were soaking, as was all the furniture. Nothing had escaped. Books, clothes, newspapers, household documents, photographs had all been damaged beyond repair. And the place was already beginning to smell. When Dad pulled back one of the carpets, we could all see that the floorboards were also well and truly soaked. Water, that giver of life, can be so destructive; poor old Arthur Hart never went back to that house.

With his usual good-natured willingness to help, Dad agreed to lend a hand sorting out the mess. In fact, Dad and I ended up doing everything by ourselves. Arthur would make arrangements to come at such-and-such a time on such-and-such a day so Dad and I would go round a bit earlier and get started. But Arthur never turned up. Not once. Why Dad continued to 'help' I don't know, but he was just that kind of man. Nothing was too much trouble if people were in need. He really was one of Nature's gentlemen, and Arthur was definitely in need.

For the next few weeks every Sunday (Dad's only day off) we pulled up the carpets, scrubbed the wallpaper off the walls, heaved the furniture out into the back yard, mopped up puddles of water that stubbornly refused to dry up of their own accord and generally worked our guts out.

Now and then Mum would turn up with biscuits and flasks of tea as the electricity and gas had been turned off, presumably as some kind of safety measure. When the tea arrived Dad would sit down on the floor, light a fag and we would have a little break.

During one of these breaks I started looking through a pile of old books which had had a proper soaking but which, although stained a dirty sort of brown, were now at least dry. There were a couple of books on holidaying in Scotland, a complete set of encyclopaedias published just after the First World War and a beautifully bound complete set of Dickens. Beneath this lot were a couple of school textbooks which had presumably been used by Edna, Arthur's daughter, when she was a pupil at one of Liverpool's grammar schools. There was a French reader, a Latin grammar and, believe it or not, a slim volume called *Hugo's Russian in Three Months*. God knows why this Liverpool plod should have a Russian grammar among his belongings, but he did. I grabbed it, opened it and started avidly reading the first section on the alphabet. Later, when we were packing up for the day, Dad said it would be all right if I borrowed it and was sure Arthur wouldn't mind. When we next saw Arthur and I asked if I could borrow it he said he didn't know anything about any Russian book in his house but added that I could help myself to anything I wanted. He had decided to stay at his daughter's and as soon as the house dried out completely he was going to move out. I don't think I ever saw him again. We had lost a neighbour but I had gained my first Russian grammar book.

Of course the mid-fifties was not a particularly good time to flaunt an interest in things Russian. Friends and relatives alike immediately associated the language with the political system and just could not understand that it was possible to be interested in Russian and not be at least a closet Commie. Suspicion even arose within my own family. Nan boasted of being an avowed socialist but said she hated Communism, and when I dared to point out that the difference was merely one of degree . . . well, it was almost like expressing a death-wish. Even Granddad, normally a tolerant and reasonable man, warned me off and tried to persuade me to learn Spanish instead, as, he argued, it had a lot of commercial potential because of the produce that came to Britain from South America via Liverpool.

But Mum was a different story. She was dead set against it. But then she was dead set against almost any ideas I had. She basically could not understand anyone wanting to study any foreign language. Russian she associated with Communism, German with Fascism and the war, Spanish and Latin with the Catholics and Italian with pasta and wine that tasted like vinegar.

'I don't want you learning any of these funny languages,' she said to me one Saturday afternoon when she was dragging me round Liverpool on a shopping expedition. 'I want you to get out of Warbreck and start studying to be a doctor. Why do you think we called you Alexander?'

This stumped me. I had always thought I was named after all the other Alexanders in the family as it was virtually a family tradition for at least one member of each generation to bear the name.

'What's my name got to do with being a doctor?' I asked, somewhat perplexed.

'You're called Alexander because I thought "Dr Alexander Tulloch" would look good on a brass plate outside your surgery.'

So the secret was out. My future had been decided for me within days of my being born and my mother wasn't my mother after all: she was the Goddess of Pre-destination.

'But I don't want to be a doctor,' I protested.

'Of course you do. Michael Melia's mum's decided he's going to be a dentist so you're going to be a doctor. If you want to learn a language you can carry on with your French so you can read a menu in a posh restaurant.'

I said nothing. I did not consider Coopers delicatessen department to be the most suitable place for a lively discussion on the subject. But inside I was seething. Surely she couldn't be serious? Surely she didn't expect me to spend years learning French just to be able to read a menu in a poncy restaurant? And as for being a doctor, she knew what she could do with that idea.

The problem was that this discussion coincided with my growing up. The hormones were kicking in and my testosterone was starting to cause problems. Whereas I had always tended to do as I was told, I was now starting to rebel a little. When we got home she got a bit of a shock.

As soon as we walked through the door I let her have it.

'Listen,' I said, 'I don't want to be a doctor and nothing you do or say will make me. For a start I'm not even at a grammar school doing the right subjects, and even if I was I wouldn't want to be a doctor.'

The look in her eyes was unbelievable. Anger and amazement seemed to fuse into a strange stare which I had never seen before.

'And if I do pass the "Thirteen Plus" I'm going to try to get into university to study languages.'

She was stunned. She couldn't understand how anyone could be interested in languages, just as, for her, anything to do with literature, poetry or art was a complete waste of time.

Young males, once the hormones take over, are supposed to rebel against their fathers, but I never did. I don't ever remember having an argument with my father; he was far too reasonable and always able to look at problems calmly and not get hot under the collar about anything. If he had a row with Mum he never raised his voice. He just calmly said what had to be said and left it at that. If Mum decided to indulge in some histrionics that was her choice, but nobody ever disturbed Dad's self-control.

So my rebelliousness was directed against my mother. She laid down all the laws in our house so she was the one who had to deal with it when people put forward ideas which differed from her own. For now the argument between her and me was over what I was going to do with my life. But over the next few years the list of potential flashpoints got longer and longer.

12

Footballs & Jam Jars

Monsieur Matheson only stayed at Warbreck for a year. After that he went off to another teaching position at Arnott Street a few miles down the road. If the grapevine was right he didn't stay there long either, but gave up teaching altogether as he found out he could make more money as a racing tipster.

Unfortunately for me, Monsieur Matheson's departure meant the end of French lessons. But it didn't really bother me unduly for two reasons: in the first place I now had a fair understanding of how to go about learning a language and, in the second, I had really become gripped by Russian and was desperately trying to teach myself from any basic textbooks I could lay my hands on. But there was also a third reason: the Thirteen Plus exam.

Liverpool was a little unusual in that it offered those who had failed the Eleven Plus a second chance two years later. And my new teacher in my second year at Warbreck laid it on the line.

'Listen, Tulloch,' said Mr Sim, 'if you want to take languages any further you have got to pass the Thirteen Plus. If you don't get to a grammar school you'll never get anywhere with your French or Russian or whatever. Concentrate on your maths and English. That's what you need for the exam so for one year you should work at them.' It was good advice and I listened to it.

From September 1956 to the scholarship exam in February of the following year Mr Sim and I got on like a house on fire . . . well, most of the time. He was one of the old school and insisted on a thorough knowledge of the basics. Punctuation and grammar were drummed into us and every Friday morning we had to write out a chapter of *Treasure Island* in our best handwriting.

Then there were the sums. God, they were awful! Bad enough in decimal times, but in the pre-decimal era they were an absolute nightmare. How on earth did we cope with monsters like this before calculators:

If a loaf of bread costs 4¾*d* how many can I buy for *£3 17s 6d*?

Or

A man wants to paper a room which measures 8ft 6in × 10ft 4in × 7ft. If a roll of wallpaper measures 12ft × 1ft 6in, how many rolls will he need? And if each roll costs 12*s* 6*d*, how much will it cost him to paper three-quarters of the room?

Now as I say, George Sim and I got on like a house on fire most, but by no means all, of the time. There was one major point on which we disagreed: sport. He was a keen sportsman and I was not. It was as simple as that. He thought running around a football pitch kicking (or, as in my case, not kicking) a football was an enjoyable way to pass an hour or two on a Wednesday afternoon. I disagreed.

'Come on, Tulloch!' I can hear him now, yelling at me from the sidelines.'Tackle him!'

More often than not the person I was being cajoled into tackling was Ronnie Everstead, a powerfully built lad with a bull neck and muscular legs many a fully grown man would have been proud to own. On the rare occasions when I did summon up the courage to tackle him I was swatted aside like an irksome fly and ended up flat on my back. Then Mr Sim's honeyed words caressed my sensitive eardrums again:

'Get up, Tulloch, you're not hurt! Don't be such a sissie! He hardly touched you!'

On such occasions it was not unknown for me to express my disagreement with Mr Sim's assessment of my physical injuries in colourful language. On such occasions also, had I expressed myself in anything above an inaudible whisper, Mr Sim would have realised that my linguistic interests now included Anglo-Saxon, in which I was capable of demonstrating a remarkably precocious fluency.

But once, only once, I was hero of the match. It was a very, very rare experience for me even to be on the winning side, let alone contribute to a victory. There was something about me and goals: we just seemed to despise each other and avoid each other's company at all costs. No matter how good a team was normally, if I was playing with them it was a foregone conclusion that they would lose. But there was one exception to this rule.

Warbreck Secondary Modern was divided up into houses like the toffee-nosed public schools. The person responsible for this was a certain Lewis W. Lewis MA, who had been headmaster back in the 1920s. He obviously wanted to give the pupils a taste of the classical education none of them would ever be exposed to by naming the four houses Romans, Trojans, Greeks and Spartans.

I was a Trojan and we were playing against the Romans on the memorable day when I left the field of battle covered in mud and glory. By some absolute fluke five minutes into the game the ball came in my direction and I just booted it. I had no idea if I was even facing the right way or not: I just saw the ball (a sodden wet dumpling of saturated leather) and kicked it. To my amazement the next thing I heard was loud cheering and I was being patted on the back by my team-mates. I had actually scored. I had scored a goal, probably for the first time in my life. But there was more to come.

By half-time some of the lustre had worn off my dazzling performance. We had been leading 1–0 for about twenty minutes but then somebody (I think it was Billy Rimmer, but I could be wrong) equalised just before half-time.

The situation remained unchanged for almost the whole of the second half. Then with literally seconds to go I scored a brilliant header. Nobody had ever seen the like before. Tulloch was finally displaying his genius and hidden talent for the beautiful game. Again I just caught sight of the ball, this time about five foot off the ground, and hurled myself at it, giving my neck an expert flick at the crucial moment, and buried the ball deep in the Romans' net. The cheers went up and I was carried shoulder high off the pitch. Had I scored one goal it would have been cause to celebrate, but I had scored two and single-handedly crushed the enemy. The admiration and appreciation of my peers was a heady brew that left me reeling with ecstasy and excitement. The adulation was mine to savour and savour it I did.

How all this came about I never did know, as the truth of the matter is a little different. I hadn't found the ball; the ball found me. My mind was not on the game at all; my apathy for the game was so total that I didn't care who won or lost. I was daydreaming about something or other and got the fright of my life when I suddenly saw this cannonball hurtling towards me at head height. I jumped to get out of its way but totally miscalculated the time–space coordinates and it hit me smack on the left ear. When my brain eventually found its way back into my skull I realised that the ball had ricocheted off my head straight into the opponents' net.

But it still counted as a goal. We had won. All the adulation and the look of sheer amazement on Mr Sim's face meant that there was no way I was going to tell anybody what really happened. If they all thought I was a hero, that was good enough for me.

Mr Sim (the second teacher who had an enormous effect on my life) had a side to him none of us had expected. We knew him as an excellent teacher who stood no messing from the boys, either in the classroom or on the football field. Firm but fair is probably the best way of describing him. But none of us knew of, or even suspected, his private passion.

The mid-fifties was the era of rock 'n' roll. American pop singers such as Elvis Presley, the pianist Fats Domino and the kiss-curled Bill Haley and his Comets suddenly burst on the scene, ousting the crooners like Bing Crosby and Frank Sinatra. Then came all the Brits, taking a leaf out of their American counterparts' book: Billy Fury, Cliff Richard and the Shadows, Adam Faith and many, many more too numerous to mention.

Of course this new music was the sole preserve of the young. Parents cringed as they watched Elvis and his British lookalikes gyrate suggestively on the television sets which were gradually invading every home in the country. The older generation neither understood nor appreciated the new music, and either condemned it outright as a cacophonous outrage or totally ignored it.

So it came as a bit of a shock when Mr Sim came into the classroom one day carrying a portable gramophone and a few vinyl 78s.

'Quiet!' he said, addressing the class, and we all shut up; you didn't disobey Mr Sim.

'Now listen to these two records and tell me what the difference is.'

He put the first record on the turntable and we couldn't believe our ears. Out of the speaker came the words which were on every teenager's lips at the time:

One, two, three o'clock, four o'clock rock,
Five, six, seven o'clock, eight o'clock rock,
Nine, ten, eleven o'clock, twelve o'clock rock
We're gonna rock around the clock to-night . . .

We sat and listened in silent amazement. Mr Sim stopped the gramophone (or record player, as we were now starting to call these machines), removed the record and replaced it with another. It was the same song but there was one vital difference. On the first one, before the opening bars, you could just make out the faint sounds of Bill Haley himself tapping with his foot on the floor: 'One, two, one two three . . .'.

We could not believe it. A grown-up (and a teacher!) had gone to the trouble of buying two copies of the same record just because on one you could hear the singer tapping out the tune with his feet. Now that was a degree of dedication to contemporary culture which nobody ever expected from such a quarter!

But no discussion of Mr Sim could ever be complete without a mention of . . . jam jars. Ask any of his former pupils what they remember about him and nine out of ten will immediately reply 'jam jars'. In fact, so strong is the link in many of his former pupils' minds between George and his jam jars that when he retired in the seventies he was presented, not with the traditional clock, but a jam jar mounted on a polished base. Not for nothing did we call him 'Jam-jar George'.

The reason for this strange association is quite simple. In those days it was not uncommon for anyone who wanted to raise a few coppers to save up used jam and marmalade jars and take them to Hartleys jam factory down Long Lane. There you could get a penny per clean jar and, although it seems a paltry amount today, a dozen could bring in a shilling, which would double the average lad's weekly pocket money.

But George Sim didn't do things by halves. The school needed some extra cash to buy additional gym equipment and George decided he would raise the money by presenting Hartleys with what was probably the greatest number of jam jars that had ever been returned to them. Not just a few rescued from the bin-men's lorry, but hundreds if not thousands of them mopped up in a swoop on the nearby streets of which any army commander could have justifiably felt proud.

How did he accomplish this feat? By organising a massive, military-style operation. George had been in the RAF for a while, so understood the importance of detailed planning if an operation were to be a success. He therefore dragooned as many of the staff as possible into the operation, as well as just about every able-bodied lad in the school. We were then sectioned off into work parties and assigned a certain number of streets in the Aintree and Fazakerley areas. Night after night as soon as school finished we all had to invade our designated areas, supervised by a member of staff, knocking on doors and asking the residents if they had any jam jars they wanted to get rid of.

The booty was then brought back to Warbreck and stored in an enormous holding area in one corner of the playground. My memory is of thousands of jam jars in a corner of the playground which eventually found their way to Hartleys factory, about a mile from the school. I suppose our efforts paid off and the new sporting gear arrived, but I can't be sure. It probably appeared after I left.

But the real business of the academic year 1956/7 was not football, Bill Haley or the jam jars saga. The real business of the year was the Thirteen Plus Scholarship exam. We slogged away all year at the basics: arithmetic, English, handwriting and so on, and no quarter was given and none asked. Mr Sim loaded the work on to us and, as far as I remember, nobody objected. We all knew what was at stake: our future. And we all knew that the Liverpool Education Authority had just opened a new grammar school, so that there were now about a hundred extra places to be fought for. Overall it probably increased the odds of getting into a grammar school only slightly, but it was enough to make us try just that little bit harder.

As the day before the exam drew to its close Mr Sim knew that he had done his best but now it was up to us. At home time he wished us all the best and made other pleasant noises to try to put us at our ease while not forgetting the importance of the day.

I was one of the last to file past him on my way out and, just as I drew level with him, he stopped me. Then he grabbed hold of my lapels and whispered what sounded like encouragement tinged with menace.

'If you let me down tomorrow, Tulloch, I'll use your head for a football on Saturday morning.' I never did find out if he was only joking.

The sun rose on the day of the Scholarship exam. The sun set on the day of the Scholarship exam. And in between these two cosmic events I travelled to the Commercial School in Evered Avenue and sat the Thirteen Plus.

And I passed.

13

Forbidden Fruit

Secondary education in those days, as I have already mentioned, was character-ised by its divisiveness. Not only were the academically more capable pupils divided from their less gifted contemporaries, but it was also decreed that, as far as was humanly possible, male should not come into contact with female. But this division of the sexes merely reflected the prevailing social attitudes evidenced elsewhere in society. The swimming baths at Queen's Drive had a men's pool and a women's pool; in the Methodist church at the top of Cedar Road there were sep-arate pews for men and women. And it was totally unthinkable that men and women should go to the same establishment to have their hair done.

And Warbreck School was no exception. There were girls at the school but between the hours of 9 a.m. and 4 p.m. we were never allowed to meet. The girls' and boys' departments were side by side but each was cloistered from the other and existed in a monastic bubble. Such isolation applied to the staff as well, as we had only men teachers and the girls had only women. In my two years at Warbreck I don't think I ever met, and certainly could not name, the headmistress or any of the women teachers who spent most of the waking hours from Monday to Friday just the thickness of a wall away from us.

The school even operated a curious system for morning assembly. Across the playground was a two-storey building which had at one time (in the thirties, I believe) housed a swimming pool on the ground floor and an assembly hall above. For some reason the swimming pool had been closed down and boarded over and converted into a second assembly hall. God knows why, but the girls' and boys' departments used to alternate between the two for morning assembly. One week the boys would be on the upper floor and the girls on the lower, the next week the girls were upstairs and we were downstairs. But such was the secrecy surrounding our respective existences that we never saw each other when we were being ushered by the teaching staff into whichever hall we had the use of in any given week.

A seven-foot-high wall separated us boys from the girls. Officially we never saw them and, I think, were supposed to pretend that they did not even exist. But we had other ideas. Purely out of curiosity we wanted to know who or what these strange creatures were whom we could hear over the wall during playtime or when a PT (physical training) class was taking place. Like sirens they tempted us with their strangely beautiful voices and, like the sailors of the Homeric epics, we found ourselves irresistibly drawn in their direction.

Normally our curiosity and daring were tempered by the knowledge that any attempt to make contact with the beings over the wall would bring down the wrath, if not of the gods, then certainly of the headmaster. But one day a few of us let temptation get the better of us. Fortunately (or unfortunately, depending on your point of view) the caretaker, Mr Bimson, had left some wooden boxes near the wall which separated us from the objects of our attention.

I think it was Alfie Burns who goaded me: 'Go on, Tulloch, let's see ya climb up an' 'av a look over into the girls' school.'

I confess I did not need much coaxing. I clambered up on to the boxes like a monkey and hooked my elbows over the wall to steady myself. It was like peeking over the wall surrounding the Garden of Eden. There in front of me were these beautiful creatures in their gymslips, running about chasing a ball, shrieking and laughing. One girl in particular caught my attention. She appeared to be slightly taller than the rest and had long blond hair. Even from the distance I could see that she had the bluest eyes I had ever seen. Quite simply, she was gorgeous. But I never saw her again.

It was while I stood there on top of the boxes, hormones all haywire, that I learned a valuable lesson. I was enchanted by the vision before me and just stared at this lovely girl, totally oblivious of the world around me. Then suddenly reality brought me down to earth with a bump, literally and figuratively. The boxes, on which I was precariously balanced, slipped and toppled over. I came crashing down with them and ended up on the ground, lying face down in an enormous puddle. I suppose it was my first lesson in the importance of metaphor: you can fall for the girls but they can also be the cause of your downfall.

Of course, all my friends were most solicitous for my well-being when they saw what had happened to me. In fact, they were so concerned for my health that they doubled up with uncontrollable laughter. Within seconds what seemed like half the school population had gathered to witness Tulloch's misery and embarrassment as he picked himself up, soaking wet and with blood trickling from his grazed knees. Unfortunately for me, among the onlookers was Mr Stein, one of the strictest teachers in the school. He asked me if I was all right, simultaneously sliding the cane out of his jacket sleeve, and when he was sure I had suffered no lasting damage, told me to hold my hand out and whacked it.

I made my way back to the classroom, soaking wet and filthy, with my knees bleeding and my right hand smarting. Not one of my happiest days at Warbreck.

Nor did things get any better when I got home. Mum was not best pleased at the sight of my filthy school shirt and blazer. And when she asked why I had come home in such a mess she hit the roof. Any self-respecting twelve-year-old should have been able to invent some cock-and-bull story to cover up his misdemeanour, but not me. I stupidly told the truth and paid the price for it.

Granddad roared with laughter and thought I was obviously going to have what he considered the right attitude towards members of the opposite sex. Strangely enough, so did Nan. But Mum thought I had committed some cardinal sin (not that she would have ever used such an expression, so redolent is it of Catholicism) by daring to look at a girl. It was all right for her to giggle lasciviously and suggestively with my sister about their screen idols, but for me other rules applied.

'You'd no business looking into the girls' playground,' she said, nervously flicking the ash from her cigarette into the ashtray. 'I think it's time your Dad had a few words with you.'

'Here it comes,' I thought to myself, 'the birds-and-bees talk.'

'What about?' I asked nonchalantly and with as convincing an air of innocence as I could manage.

'Never you mind,' she replied, now nervously taking another fag out of its packet and lighting it. 'It's just time for you to have a talk to your Dad about . . . things.'

'What things?' I asked, maintaining the same malicious pretence of innocence.

'Your Dad can explain when he comes in,' she said as she put her coat on and claimed to have to nip round to Oddy's the greengrocers for some carrots.

'Why are you blushing, Mum?' I could not resist teasing her.

'I'm not blushing,' she protested. 'I've probably just put too much rouge on.'

With that she disappeared out of the back door into the dark, foggy night.

When Dad did come home nothing was said. I was in the sitting room trying to do my homework but I could not really concentrate as I expected to be summoned for the talk 'about . . . things'. But the call never came. There was a lot of whispering from the kitchen, then just the hint of raised voices followed by total silence.

The conclusion I drew from all this was that Dad had been briefed on my antics at school and given his orders to give me a lecture on the meaning of life and all that, but that he had refused. Whatever the reason, the talk did not happen. In fact, it never happened. And I'm glad, really. It was far more fun finding out for myself.

14

Keeping Mum

Dad's reluctance and Mum's embarrassment when it came to talking about certain matters was not their fault. They were born (1907 and 1916 respectively) at a time when Queen Victoria's influence was still felt. People tend to think that 'Victorian attitudes' ended with the old Queen's death in 1901, but this is not the case. For decades afterwards people shied away from almost anything to do with the two great inevitables, birth and death. In a similar way people hardly ever mentioned the word 'cancer'. Nobody was ever said to have cancer. It was merely observed, almost in passing, that so-and-so was 'getting thin now' or that 'he's got a growth'.

Nor did any woman ever get pregnant. Married women were merely referred to, with almost the same passing nonchalance, as 'getting bigger'. In the case of unmarried girls who found themselves in an 'interesting condition', their predicament was hardly ever mentioned but they would suddenly and mysteriously disappear. After a while their absence would be explained as an unexpected need for a long holiday or the offer of a job in another town. The truth was more likely to be that they had been shunted away somewhere to be looked after by nuns who would then persuade (or should that be 'force'?) them to offer their newly born son or daughter up for adoption.

By an unfortunate twist of fortune Mum was the victim of what might be described as a coincidence of the unmentionables. In 1958 my sister decided that she wanted to get married. She had been going out with Bill (her 'intended', as my grandmother described him) for a couple of years and they had come to the conclusion that it was time to tie the knot. With her characteristic flair for taking charge (some would have said 'interference'), she took Marg to the jeweller's to choose the engagement ring. Some might have expected the future bride and groom to undertake this intimate task, but not Mum. She was unshakably convinced that only she would be capable of buying the right ring at the right price and never even considered that the two love-birds might actually like to have a say in what kind of ring they wanted to buy. And, to crown it all, she even chose their wedding ring a few months later!

But matters didn't end there. With most couples the future husband takes it on himself to arrange, book and pay for the honeymoon. But once again Mum thought that nobody could be trusted to make such a momentous decision apart from herself. So she booked them a room in the Craig-Ard, the hotel in Llandudno where

The author and his father in the front garden of the Craig-Ard Hotel, Llandudno, in 1955. *(Author's collection)*

we had been as a family a couple of times, for a few days following the wedding which she set for 12 November 1958.

It seemed that everything was set in stone. The date was fixed, the wedding arranged, the ring bought and the honeymoon venue decided. So it came as a bit of a shock when my sister came home from work one day to be told by my mother that she had cancelled everything. Yes, she had. Without so much as a by-your-leave or even discussing it with the principal players in this farce, she had cancelled the arrangements and simply presented Marg with a *fait accompli*.

'Why?' said my sister, understandably feeling slightly miffed.

'Never mind. It's got nothing to do with you.'

'Nothing to do with me? How can it have nothing to do with me? It's Bill and me who are getting married!'

'Listen, Madam [a term she always used when addressing any woman who was trying her patience]. It's just not convenient for Jack and Vi coming down from Edinburgh. I've changed everything so you're getting married on September 11th.'

'Yes, but . . .', my sister began.

'No buts about it,' came the lightning-flash retort. Then she added, almost as an afterthought, 'And besides, Granddad isn't very well. We think he might have TB.'

But he didn't have TB. He had lung cancer. His sudden weight loss, shortness of breath and constant coughing had just been confirmed as symptoms of the Big C, but Mum could not bring herself to mention the word. It was almost as if cancer was seen as some kind of socially unacceptable or even shameful disease which might have been prevented by a more temperate lifestyle.

The Craig-Ard Hotel and front garden as they are today. *(By kind permission of David Gee, hotel proprietor)*

So Mum found herself on the horns of the proverbial dilemma. She had to keep the real nature of Granddad's illness a secret from everyone, even members of the family (I was never even told he was ill; I had to work it out for myself) and she had a good idea that he would not last to see his granddaughter married unless the date were brought forward by a few months. But in those days people only brought a wedding forward if it was a rush job, or 'shotgun', as such hurried affairs were generally known. So she knew the neighbours would immediately start whispering about Marg 'having to get married' and commenting on her 'getting rather big', but there was nothing she could do.

As it happened, Mum's timing was perfect. Marg and Bill did get married in September and Granddad died at the beginning of November, a few days before the date originally set for the nuptials. And, of course, within a relatively short space of time the nosey neighbours had to abandon all their tut-tutting and Chinese whispers: it was not for another three years that Marg told the world (in January 1961) that she was expecting.

Of course I was not present at the grand announcement. I wasn't even told about it until Marg was suddenly rushed into hospital with a suspected miscarriage. But even then I was only given the expurgated version of events. Mum just said she had something wrong with her tummy and she had to go into Walton Hospital for a few days rest.

What my mother didn't know, however, was that I had heard the word 'miscarriage'. I had unexpectedly walked in on one of the grown-ups' whispered conversations and heard this new word. I hadn't got a clue what it meant but casually mentioned it to a girlfriend I had at the time.

'Don't you know what a miscarriage is?' she asked in disbelief.

'No,' I replied, feeling I should be experiencing some sort of shame at my lack of knowledge in such matters.

'It means she's lost the baby,' Diane replied.

'Baby?! What baby?' I stammered.

'Don't you know anything?' she said, unable to comprehend the extent of my ignorance. 'She must have been pregnant [I blushed at her casual use of this "naughty" word] and if she's had a miscarriage it must have died in the womb [another shameful word].' She then proceeded to give me what was probably my first talk ever on the facts of life. Until then most of my information came from pure guesswork and putting together odd snippets I'd gleaned from overhearing adults' conversations or listening to older boys who knew little more than I did. And much of what they thought they knew was wrong anyway.

It seems unbelievable now but at the time of this conversation I was seventeen years old. Obviously I had known the basic facts of life for years, but the finer, more arcane aspects of childbirth were still a mystery to me. This might seem unbelievable in the twenty-first century but before the 1960s secrets were secrets and as far as children, and even teenagers, were concerned the biggest secret of all was where we all come from!

15

A Pint & a Fag

Passing the Thirteen Plus was a life-changing experience. It meant I got a smart grammar-school uniform, complete with long trousers, a peaked cap and a Latin inscription (VERITAS VINCIT, 'Truth Conquers') on the blazer badge. It also meant that my ten- or fifteen-minute walk to school every morning was replaced by a bus journey of over an hour. I now had to leave home at ten to eight, catch a bus up to Queen's Drive and then another out through Woolton and past Hunt's Cross to the glass edifice known as Hillfoot Hey High School.

However, there were also sociological effects that I had not anticipated. Most of my erstwhile friends just disappeared. Like the gases produced in the experiments we carried out in the spanking new chemistry laboratories at Hillfoot, they just seemed to vanish into thin air. The friends I had at Warbreck now saw me as some

The Co-op at the junction of Regina Road and Walton Vale. It was behind this building that the author tried smoking his first cigarette. *(Liverpool Record Office)*

snotty-nosed swot who'd rather spend his time poring over books than playing out or joining them in their tentative forays into adulthood. And such moves usually meant having a sly Woodbine behind the air-raid shelters or making yourself look old enough to get into a pub and ask for a pint of beer.

But this is where they made a big mistake. Scrapping short trousers for a grammar-school uniform did not mean that I had ditched my curiosity about the world of grown-up pleasures and predilections. Oh no. I was just as keen as anyone else to sample the pleasures of tobacco and had no hesitation whatever when June Lawson coaxed me down a back alley behind the Co-op at the top of Regina Road and produced a packet of five Capstan full strength.

'Go on,' she said. 'Our Danny smokes these all the time. Can't do you any harm.'

And as if by way of encouragement and/or seduction she took out a cigarette, struck a match against the wall and slowly brought the tulip-shaped flame up to the few strands of tobacco hanging limply from the fag which by now she was twirling between her lips. Then she gently sucked at it until the end glowed bright red and when she was sure it was well lit she took it out of her mouth, tilted her head backwards and deftly blew three or four smoke rings.

'Have you never tried it?' she asked.

'Er . . . well . . . no, not really,' I was ashamed to admit. 'But I will if you give me one.'

She was obviously not going to give me a chance to change my mind. In no time at all she had taken another fag out of the packet, lit it and put it in my mouth.

'Draw the smoke in,' she instructed me, 'then just let it swirl around your mouth. Now swallow it.'

I obeyed without question. There was no way I was going to let her think I couldn't do what the grown-ups did.

Just then we heard her father shouting down the alley. 'June! Where are ya? Yer tea's ready. Cum on in now.'

Quick as a flash and with no sign of embarrassment she lifted her dress and shoved the packet of cigarettes down inside her knickers. Then she just disappeared and left me to finish off the experimental fag.

I did finish it but very soon regretted it. First of all I started coughing. Then I started to feel sick and sweaty. Next I was overcome by this need to get home as fast as I could. I was ill, really ill. The light from the street lamps started swirling round and the houses seemed to want to do the same thing. 'Oh God,' I thought, 'I'm dying . . . Mum! . . . Dad! . . . Quick!!'

'Are ya all right, lad?' was the next thing I heard. I could feel the cold, hard pavement underneath me and saw this unfamiliar face staring down at me out of the darkness.

'What's de matter wid ya? It looks like y've been sick. Tell us where ya live and I'll take yer 'ome.'

'No thanks,' I said. 'I'll be OK.'

There was no way I wanted anybody at home to know what I'd been up to. Anyway, by now I was feeling much better, if a little groggy on my feet. So I just thanked the stranger and made my way home, first stopping under a street lamp to make sure none of the vomit had stuck to my clothes.

I can't think why, but for some reason it was a long time before I tried smoking a cigarette again.

The results were similar but not quite so dramatic when I decided to have a go at the other adult pastime: drinking beer.

I was about fifteen years old and had been to some function in the centre of Liverpool organised for the city's grammar-school pupils. On my way to the bus-stop I passed one of the many pubs which cluster around Lime Street station. Suddenly a mischievous little voice inside my head said, 'Why don't you go inside and see if you can get a pint?'

I had never been inside a pub before in my life, let alone asked for a pint of beer. So where this voice came from I could not even hazard a guess. But come it did. At first I ignored it but then it started repeating itself over and over again until I finally thought, 'Oh well, let's just see. After all, the worst they can do is say no and throw me out.'

But they didn't say no and they didn't throw me out. On the contrary, the lady behind the bar smiled beautifully as I walked in and asked what she could get me.

'Er . . . a pint of Guinness, please.'

God alone knows why I asked for a pint of Guinness. I had never tasted it and had no idea what it would be like. The only explanation I can offer is that seconds before entering the sawdust-floored boozer I had seen a huge placard opposite extolling the silky texture and unique flavour of Ireland's most famous export.

Suddenly, as if sent from heaven, there it was on the bar in front of me – a pint of a dark, sultry liquid topped with a pure white froth nearly an inch deep. The glass looked me straight in the eye, brazenly tempting me to pick it up, sip the velvet nectar within and surrender my taproom virginity. I was hypnotised by its sensual appeal and gradually became aware of my hand sliding over its warm surface and taking a firm grip of its beautifully curved form. I raised it slowly to my lips and, shaking with anticipation, took a gentle swig . . . it tasted awful. It was bitter and slimy and, to my mind, totally failed to live up to its tempting promises. But my manhood was at stake. I did not want the other people in the pub to see me push the glass away. Not only would I be admitting defeat but it would have been a dead give-away to even the most casual observer that this was my first attempt at crossing the line from childhood into the world of the adult. So I had to finish it. It took me the best part of an hour but I managed it.

At least it didn't make me sick. No. In fact quite the opposite. When I emerged from the pub I was feeling just a little light-headed and in a very, shall we say, jaunty mood. To tell the truth, so jaunty was my mood that I skipped along Lime Street, alternately whistling and singing so that one or two passers-by questioned me on my fortuitous discovery:

'Looks like good ale, that, la'. Which boozer did ya gerrid in?'

I had no idea of the pub's name so I just waved at them and grinned like a demented Cheshire cat then continued my merry (very merry!) way in a vaguely homeward direction.

Booze and fags apart, the effects of passing the Thirteen Plus did have a more serious side. As I say, to many people I suddenly became a toffee-nosed grammar-school kid, although I was not aware of any change in myself at all. Kids I used to hang around with on street corners or played rally-o with or cricket using a lamp-post as the wickets just didn't want to know me. As soon as they saw me coming towards them they would start making unkind comments, telling me to get lost or asking if I hadn't got any homework I should be doing. What I could never understand was that some of the former friends who were most enthusiastic in their jeering were lads who had passed the Eleven Plus and had already been at a grammar school for at least two years. Perhaps the magic had worn off for them and so they were somewhat irritated by my still-evident excitement at being able to prove to the world that I was not the academic duffer everybody had previously thought I was.

But I was not going to dwell on the sociological and psychological effects of my transfer to Hillfoot for too long. If I had to find new friends, so be it. That is exactly what I did.

16

French Leave

Hillfoot was very different from Warbreck. For a start most of the teachers wore academic gowns (Mr Pomfret, the Spanish master, boasted that his tattered old gown was over a hundred years old and that he had inherited it from his grandfather) and this somehow gave them an aura of authority which Warbreck teachers lacked. And if a gown lent an aura of authority to its wearer, none looked more impressive than the headmaster, Mr Dunn. A towering six foot four mountain of a man, he would battleship down the corridors smoking his pipe (it was allowed in those days) making sure none of his charges was up to no good or in a place where the timetable decreed he ought not to be. By coincidence Mr Dunn's Christian name was Edward, and this was seized upon by the Liverpool wits in the school so that Edward the Head soon became known simply as 'The 'Eddie'.

Hillfoot Hey High School, Woolton, was built in the 1950s and demolished in the 1970s. The land is now occupied by a private housing estate. (*Liverpool Record Office*)

The other main difference with Warbreck was that the staff stayed in their rooms and the pupils were (to use a new word we all learned on the first day) 'peripatetic'. We now had so many different teachers for the different subjects that we had to carry around bulging schoolbags with textbooks for maths, physics, chemistry, Spanish, English and even woodwork.

The educational ethos of Hillfoot was, understandably, that of a traditional grammar school. Although it was only opened in 1956, none of the new-fangled ideas which were to plague education within a matter of a few years influenced the subjects to be taught there. As in Alsop's, the Liverpool Institute, the Liverpool Collegiate or Quarry Bank, all long-established traditional selective institutions, the boys in Hillfoot were to be given a solid education in what in those days were considered the essentials. English lessons were heavily biased towards grammar, correct spelling and punctuation, and an ability to express oneself in clear, unambiguous language. The mind-numbing stupidity which decreed that such topics were élitist and hindered expression was still the better part of a decade away, so we were lucky enough to benefit from Mr Finney's expert tuition in such matters before the rot set in.

Languages also formed a major part of the curriculum. It seems amazing to look back now and think that Hillfoot, along with all the other state-run grammar schools in Liverpool, offered a multiplicity of foreign languages which would be unheard of today. During a four- or five-year stint at the school a pupil, if he wished, could study almost any combination of Latin, French, Spanish and German. And Mr Dunn, perceptive character that he was, called me into his study at the end of my first year at the school and made me an offer I could not refuse.

Hillfoot Hey's playground. The all-glass side to the building meant that pupils inside were almost fried alive at their desks on hot summer days. *(Liverpool Record Office)*

'Listen, Tulloch, let's be honest. Cards on the table, eh? Your only hope of making anything of yourself in this life is going to revolve around languages, isn't it?'

'Yes, Sir,' I agreed, wondering what he was leading up to.

'I mean,' he continued, scratching his bald head for a second or two, 'you'll never be a scientist, will you?'

Remembering my pathetic exam results in chemistry and physics, I could hardly protest or try to pretend that he was at that very moment involved in a conversation with a budding Newton or Einstein.

'And you're not very good at maths either, are you?'

My miserable recent exam mark flashed before my eyes. Ten per cent. Then almost at the same time I heard Mr Aiston's sarcastic remark as he handed back my paper, 'and five per cent was for getting your name right!'

Faced with all this evidence, there would have been little point in my even attempting to persuade Mr Dunn that he might have misjudged my abilities just a little.

But I'm glad I didn't because what he said next sealed my future.

'I'll let you concentrate on languages and drop the subjects you're not interested in or which you have difficulty with [there was an understatement!] if you want. You can do French and Spanish, and Mr Forbes has agreed to help you with your Russian [which I was still trying to learn by myself]. You can also keep on with history and I'm afraid you will have to plug away at maths as you have got to have either maths or a science at O level for university entrance. And if you pass these subjects you can skip the fifth form and go into the sixth. Then you can carry on with your languages to A level and I'll arrange for you to do O level Latin at the same time. What do you say?'

As if I was going to refuse an offer like that! I grabbed it with both hands. That was the kind of thing a headmaster was allowed to do back in the fifties. Now, of course, we have 'progressed' so far and those who make decisions about our educational policies would never allow such inspired spontaneity and independence of thought and action. Happy days!

Once the die was cast there was no going back. But at least when Mum was faced with the fact that no less a person than the headmaster realised that languages were going to be my bread and butter, even she had to resign herself, still reluctantly, to the bitter truth. Having a son as a linguist must have seemed a very poor substitute to having a son as a doctor, but she had to settle for it. Eventually she had to come to terms with the situation, but only grudgingly. For some reason she never accepted that a knowledge of foreign languages could be just as useful as knowing the difference between a broken tibia and a fractured fibula.

Just before Easter 1958 my interest in languages bore fruit. The French teacher, Mr Green (Harry to everyone in Hillfoot), organised a school trip to Paris. It was probably quite a burden on the family purse, but Mum and Dad offered very little, if any, resistance when I came home from school and asked if I could go. I emphasised (of course!) that Mr Green said it would do wonders for my French. So as soon as school finished for the Easter break a party of us caught the train at Lime

Street and set off on what was to be our very first trip abroad. The strange thing is, however, that I remember almost nothing about that journey. In fact the only thing I do remember with any definite clarity is the sight of Mr Jordan, the games teacher, sitting opposite me in the carriage reading *French for Beginners*. It did cross my mind that learning the language when you're already *en route* was a bit like reading *Teach Yourself to Swim* as you're leaving port on the *Titanic*.

We didn't actually stay in Paris. Mr Green had organised accommodation for us in a school in Versailles, just across the road from the beautiful famous chateau. Wonderful! Well, yes, fine but not for the reasons you might expect. The reason we were all so thrilled to be in Versailles was the girl who served us in the archetypal French café just around the corner. This vision of delight greeted us every evening with a disarming smile that made us all go weak at the knees. And her pleasant manner, combined with the fact that we could legally buy and drink as much beer as we could hold, made the educational purposes of the trip slip somewhat into the background. After all, for a group of adolescent lads getting their first taste of relative freedom abroad the attractions of the Palace of Versailles or the history of the Louvre did not seem all that important. The theory behind the trip was presumably that it would broaden our minds and be good for our souls, but our minds and souls were the last thing we were concerned about. Looking at the *Mona Lisa* might be educationally instructive and being slowly taken up in the lift to the top of the Eiffel Tower might be a breathtaking experience, and strolling down the Champs-Elysées like a Hollywood film star might be something to impress our mums with when we got home. But we were more interested in staring through an alcohol-induced haze at the flesh-and-blood creation who turned us all to jelly simply by saying '*Bonsoir*' and then asking '*De la bière?*' At such moments, what red-blooded fifteen-year-old, particularly one who any day now might have to start shaving, would think of the O level exams on the distant horizon?

But if every cloud has a silver lining then a silver lining can also have a cloud. And this particular cloud came in the shape of scar-faced thug who turned up in the café one night to set the record straight. For some reason I found myself in the café by myself on that occasion and was half-way through my first beer when he made what can only be described as a dramatic entrance. A quick glance around the bar and he knew who he wanted to speak to . . . me. He spoke no English and my schoolboy French was by no means equal to the task of following his every word. I certainly caught the gist of what he was saying, but this was not so much a testament to the excellence of my spoken French as evidence of the value of gut feeling and primitive survival instincts. This turned out to be one of those occasions when language is superfluous. Some of his more interesting grammatical structures might have eluded me but there was no doubting the essence of what he was trying to say. I suspect, however, that his excellent communication skills also had something to do with the gleaming flick-knife which he suddenly produced and the hand gestures which suggested that he and the charming girl were more than 'just good friends'.

'Oh well,' I thought on my way back to the Lycée, 'she wasn't all that good-looking, anyway.'

Most of the time during our stay we were all kept together and conducted on the usual touristy sight-seeing trips. We went up to Montmartre, saw Napoleon's tomb, visited the Eiffel Tower and gazed with feigned interest at the Arc de Triomphe. But we did manage some time to wander off on our own. And it was during one of these 'free periods' that I had an encounter which I have never forgotten.

I called in to a café right by Notre Dame, itching to try out my French again by ordering a coffee and something to eat. In front of me was an American who was trying his valiant best to buy a cup of coffee and a slice of something sweet. Hesitantly and obviously groping for the words he eventually worked out what he had to say, 'Er . . . *Un . . . une . . . un café . . . avec . . .* oh gee no . . . *à lait . . .* no . . . *au lait.*'

'*Oui, monsieur,*' answered the infinitely patient, moustachioed waiter, '*et est-ce que vous voulez du gâteau aussi?*'

The poor Yank looked dazed. He hadn't got the faintest idea what the waiter had said to him. He looked just as perplexed when the waiter asked him again.

'Excuse me,' I said, interrupting, 'would you like me to help you? He's asking if you would like a slice of cake as well.'

The American looked most relieved and, after picking up his coffee and apple cake, turned to me and said in what sounded to me like a Texan drawl, 'Gee, thanks, pal, I thought I was never going to get this coffee.'

I then asked for my coffee and something to go with it, picked them up and went and sat down. The Yank saw where I was sitting and came over to join me and we struck up a conversation.

I was right about the drawl; he was from Texas. At first we chatted about this and that and nothing in particular. But fairly soon the conversation turned towards specifics and you can imagine my surprise when, after telling him what I was doing in Paris, I asked what he did back home in the States and he replied nonchalantly, 'Me? I teach French in a high school.'

17

Liverpool Wanderers

It is impossible for anyone born since 1970 to understand the word 'smog'. He or she has quite possibly experienced mist and may have had some occasional dealing with fog. But smog is something which had to be experienced first hand to be fully appreciated.

Before the Clean Air Act of the 1960s most industrial towns in these islands suffered, as regular as clockwork, weeks of dense smog that descended over them in the winter months. The very word 'smog' was a hybrid of two others: 'smoke' and 'fog', as these were the two components of the atmospheric conditions that brought most of the country to a standstill for a couple of weeks every year. And they were not only inconvenient; they were deadly. It is no exaggeration to say that every year, countrywide, several hundreds if not thousands of people died. Those suffering from asthma and bronchitis were particularly at risk, and when the smogs arrived they were warned to stay indoors and keep warm.

And Liverpool was no exception. These 'pea-soupers', as they were known, were the pernicious legacy of the Industrial Revolution. The north-west of England in

A collection of trams at the Pier Head in 1947. *(Sutton Collection)*

those days was home to much heavy industry which belched out thousands of tons of smoke from its chimneys every year. Central heating was unheard of in houses and so they, too, added to the toxic concoction by burning coal fires and adding to the clouds of thick black foul-smelling smoke which drifted up into the atmosphere. For most of the year all these emanations floated skywards, but in winter (October and November in particular I seem to remember) the smoke combined with the seasonal mists and fog and fell back to earth, covering it with an impenetrable, lethal blanket.

Driving in such conditions was well-nigh impossible. Again, only those who have experienced it can imagine how difficult it was to see where you were going. It was bad enough on foot when visibility was down to just a few yards or even inches. Then the worst that could happen was that a pedestrian might lose his way or fall and perhaps break a bone. Driving a car in these conditions, on the other hand, was quite simply suicidal. And that was just in the daytime! Imagine what it was like when the smog enveloped a town so that you could not see the person standing right next to you and then factor in the darkness of a winter evening. When things were this bad the transport authorities had no choice: they took the buses and trams off the roads until the smog cleared.

The only trouble with this arrangement was that the smog sometimes did not clear. And, unfortunately, the smog had this nasty habit of descending at about three o'clock in the afternoon, just in time to settle in before people started leaving offices, factories and schools and heading home. The consequence was that Liverpool and, I'm sure, many other towns and cities throughout the country became a city of wandering ghosts gliding eerily through dense clouds impenetrable even to the most powerful street-lamps and trying to return to their wives, their husbands, their lovers and children.

Fortunately we were usually let out of school early so that we could get the bus at least for the greater part of the journey. One day, however, I remember the head calling the school together in the assembly hall at about three o'clock. The smog had come down with even greater rapidity than usual and had caught everyone by surprise.

'I'm not going to detain you any longer than necessary. The rest of lessons for today are cancelled. You are to leave the school now and make your way home.'

He then said a few words about safety and watching out for cars that sometimes mounted the pavements when visibility was so bad. We were then dismissed and told to begin our long trek homewards. Some of the pupils lived fairly close to the school, so it wasn't too bad for them. Others lived a bit further away and would be sitting in front of a roaring fire enjoying a hot drink within no more than about half an hour. But Buddy Reid, Dave Hartley, Peter Kvalen, Dave Rimmer and I lived between eight and ten miles away! There was nothing else for it; we just had to point our noses in the right direction and start putting one foot in front of the other. And this is exactly what we did.

At first it was a bit of a lark. We were young, fit and healthy. Ten miles? A piece of cake! None of us doubted that, if we got a move-on we could be home in just over a couple of hours. We even ran part of the way, but we soon decided that was not the best course of action, considering we were all carrying what felt like a ton of textbooks in our satchels. No, we thought, much better to conserve our energy and not burn ourselves out in the first mile.

Walking through dense smog was no joke. After a while the acidic-tasting vapour found its way into your mouth, irritating the back of your throat and making you want to cough. It also made your eyes smart so that your natural reaction was to close them as much as possible, and this obviously made seeing where you were going even more difficult. But we had to persevere and just keep plodding on, mile after dreary mile.

The couple of hours we had estimated for the journey turned out to be wildly optimistic. As we lived at different distances from the school, some of us peeled off earlier than others. Pete Kvalen lived in Old Swan so he was one of the first to get home. Another hour and a half down the road it was my turn, but people like Dave Hartley and Buddy Reid had to walk further on as far as Fazakerley which, considering the conditions, probably added another hour to their odyssey.

I arrived home at about eight o'clock. It had taken me the better part of five hours to complete the journey! I was exhausted, frozen stiff, bedraggled and almost dead with hunger. But Dad's only comment as I walked through the door was 'Made it at last then? It's a calendar you want, not a watch.'

Sociologically there is a point here which should not be missed. Despite Dad's flippant sarcasm, he and Mum were both concerned for my whereabouts. But they understood the most likely reason for my tardy return from school. They knew the buses had stopped running and that Shanks's pony was the only way home. Not for a moment did they consider that I might have been abducted by a local paedophile or murdered by some frenzied lunatic. Can you imagine the anguish that would be caused today by a five-hour delay in getting home from school!

The other interesting observation to make here is that the experience did not seen to have any adverse effect on us. In fact just the opposite seems to have been the case. Long, gruelling walks in adverse conditions suddenly acquired a romantic appeal which a few of us found irresistible. So the next trek was not the reaction to sudden meteorological changes that meant the closure of the school, but to a few of us deciding, a couple of months later, that it would be a bit of a laugh to go off on a long hike one day. Then some bright spark (I can't remember who exactly) came up with the idea that we should make it a night-time expedition, just to add a bit of spice and make things a little more interesting. Well, it certainly did that!

The event was planned with unmilitary imprecision. It was decided that four of us would meet at the pier head at about 11 p.m. the following Friday, catch the ferry across the Mersey and then start walking, vaguely in the direction of Wales, and stay there for the whole weekend. We all had to bring sandwiches and a couple of hot flasks each for sustenance on the first night. The only other essential was enough money to buy our food and perhaps have a bit more for emergencies.

Had our military planning been just a tad more professional one of us might have had the gumption to listen to a weather forecast. But no, none of us bothered.

We were the valiant lads who had walked all the way home from Hillfoot in dense smog, so we could handle anything the Welsh countryside could throw at us. Couldn't we?

When we got off the ferry in Birkenhead we noticed that it seemed a lot colder than on the Liverpool side of the river. But we told each other that all we had to do was start walking at a brisk pace and we'd soon warm up. As it happened we did get warmer. In those pre-anorak days warm clothing consisted of several layers of vests, shirts and pullovers and an outer coat to keep us reasonably dry. I was wearing what was known as a jerkin or, more colloquially, a 'windjammer'. This was a belted jacket which zipped all the way up at the front and consequently did what it was supposed to do: it kept the wind out. But the problem was that these inelegant garments were made out of a single thin layer of rubber and the effects of this were twofold. They were absolutely useless when it came to keeping the wearer warm, as its 'tog' value (not that the term had been invented in those days) was nil. But at the same time as offering no protection against the cold it made anyone stupid enough to wear it for long periods pour with sweat. And this is precisely what happened to me. Striding out with a will warmed me up at the same time as the rubber windjammer made me sweat. But if I slowed down or stopped for a breather, my sweat-soaked vest and shirt started to freeze and this made stopping at the roadside for the odd breather a very uncomfortable experience.

Anyway, *nil desperandum*, we had a quick look at the map at the back of our Letts Schoolboys' Diary and decided to follow the signs for Mold, a little Welsh market town about twenty miles from Birkenhead in what then was still the county of Flintshire, but is now officially Denbighshire and Flintshire. It was a part of the world I was well acquainted with as I had spent some time there the year before, so it fell to my lot to be group leader.

Fortunately this was not a particularly arduous task. All it involved was the ability to read the road signs and periodically warn everybody not to get lost and to keep up with the group. Not that there was any real need to do this: there were only four of us so we were hardly like to lose sight of one another, but it made me feel as if I was carrying out my duties as group leader a bit more efficiently.

Our strategy was to head roughly south down the Wirral peninsula, along the A41 through Bebington and then on along the A550 to Queensferry, where the bridge over the River Dee drops travellers down over the border into Wales.

Everything was going fine until we reached Bebington at something between midnight and one o'clock in the morning. Just as we were leaving the town it started to snow. Then the wind got up and in no time at all we found ourselves slogging along, heads bowed, against a howling blizzard. There was nothing we could do. It wasn't as if we could just give up and catch the next bus home. We had left civilisation behind and found ourselves in the no-man's land between towns so that the only protection from the elements was the occasional bush or tree which really were no protection at all. Suddenly I found myself making mental comparisons between this trip and the hike home through the Liverpool smog. I could not decide which was worse: the motionless smog that seemed to burn the inside of my

Perhaps the most famous view of the city of Liverpool – the Liver Buildings from the river. *(Sutton Collection)* throat or the howling wind sending needle-pointed granules of ice right into my face and forehead. It was one of those times when a voice inside your head asks the question no logic can answer: 'What the hell am I doing here? I could be back at home wrapped up in a nice warm bed, so why am I doing this?'

It was Buddy Reid who brought me out of my reverie. He understood (probably better than the rest of us as he had been a scout) that we were in a potentially dangerous situation and the first thing we needed to do was get some food into our stomachs. He suggested we should just find somewhere to rest, forget the snow which by now formed a carpet and inch or two deep on the ground, and get some of the sandwiches and hot soup down our throats.

So imagine the scene. It's about three-thirty on a dark, moonless night in the middle of January. There is a howling blizzard blowing almost parallel with the ground and in the middle of nowhere sit four lads, all togged up against the biting cold, sipping boiling hot soup in an effort to get some feeling back into their legs, hands and feet. They are battling manfully against the elements, sustained not so much by their heroic determination to carry on against the odds as by the knowledge that they either finish their soup and get moving or die of exposure.

What happens next? The four lads are just finishing off their soup and sandwiches and are about to move off on the next leg of the journey. Suddenly, out of the blizzard emerges a Teddy Boy wearing nothing but the regulation drape jacket, drainpipe trousers and crêpe-soled shoes. Nothing else. No top coat of any description, which might have gone some way to keeping him warm and dry.

'What the 'ell are you doin' here?' he asked in a sing-song Welsh accent.

We were a bit stunned but answered him nevertheless, saying we were from Liverpool and were hiking into Wales for the weekend.

'You must be mad,' he said, 'coming out on a night like this.'

We looked at each other in amazement. Then one of us replied:

'Well at least we're all wrapped up and we've brought food and flasks of soup with us. Where have you come from dressed like that? Aren't you cold?'

If we were somewhat taken aback by his last statement we were floored by what he said next.

'No, I'm not cold. I've walked from Liverpool, too. I only live down the road a bit. I go to Liverpool every Friday night, 'ave a few beers with some friends an' then we go to a dance, and then I always have to walk home 'cos there's no buses. Usually I like to finish off the night by getting into a good fight but I didn't manage to tonight. Mustn't 'ave gone to the right dance-hall!'

He then tagged along with us for the last half-mile before he reached home. 'Tara then, lads,' he said good-naturedly. 'Hope you enjoy the rest of your little stroll . . . ha . . . ha!'

With that he disappeared up a garden path and in through the front door.

'Nobody will ever believe us if we tell them about him,' said Buddy. None of us disagreed.

After this brief encounter we carried on into Wales. We still had a fair old way to go, but the hot soup and tasty sandwiches put a renewed spring in our step and we marched further into the country where everybody is supposed to sing all the time and all the girls are called Blodwen.

The weather by now was really atrocious but we carried on and eventually found ourselves on the road to Buckley. We knew that once we reached it, it would only be a hop, skip and a jump to our final destination. There was an eerie feel to Buckley. We got there at about five o'clock and could just detect the first signs of life as the people of the town stirred. A milk-cart glided almost silently past us and then rattled off into the distance. There was a man trying to get his car started and another digging his out of the snow. We thought it strange that people were up and about at that ungodly hour, but I wonder what they thought as they saw four frozen spectres of humanity drift past the end of their drives at a time when most honest people are still in bed.

We walked into Mold at about six o'clock. Not surprisingly, the place was dead. Our idea was to make for the nearest café and get the other side of some bacon and eggs and a mug of tea, but there was nowhere open. We were convinced that there would at least be a transport café open, but no. Then someone had a brain-wave and suggested we try the railway station. It was just possible the buffet would be open and we could at least get a hot drink.

But no. The buffet was closed. The only thing left for us to do was get our heads down in the waiting room and this is what we did. There was absolutely nothing we could do about eating and drinking but at least we could get out of the freezing cold wind and perhaps get a bit of a kip. The next thing I remember was a stentorian voice booming in my ears.

'Now, now, what's all this then?'

It was the station-master (every station had one in those days!), who wanted to know why he had four frozen corpses asleep on the benches in his waiting room when he turned up for work. When we explained how we came to invade his territory he roared with laughter at our sorry plight but took pity on us.

'Come with me,' he said. 'You can't stay here, it's too cold. There's a roaring fire in my office and I can make you a mug of something hot.'

We could not believe our ears. Such generosity! Our faith in the eternal kindness of the human spirit had been restored and we jumped off those benches like scalded cats.

Well, not quite. That's how we should have returned to the vertical but we had a problem. We had all fallen asleep in the foetal position but were so cold that when we went to stand up again we couldn't. Our legs were frozen, bent at the knees. We couldn't straighten them. So any early-morning travellers standing on the platform of Mold station that day would have witnessed a scene from a comedy show. A tall, heavily built stationmaster was striding out down the platform, followed by four bedraggled youths struggling along in an ungainly fashion on legs which, for the time being, no amount of coaxing could straighten out.

The stationmaster was true to his word. When we eventually hobbled into his office the sight that greeted us was one of pure delight. A fire! And not just a miserable few coals in a pitiful excuse for a grate. This was a real inferno. As soon as we walked through the doors we could feel the heat flying across the room at us from the heap of coal so high that it seemed to disappear up the chimney. And almost immediately we were each holding a mug of steaming hot tea, loaded with sugar. Never, before or since, did a drink look and taste so wonderful.

When we had thawed out and bidden a fond farewell to our kindly guardian angel in a British Railways uniform we walked on into the town and, to our delight, found a café where we treated ourselves to the biggest fry-up breakfast you could imagine.

We emerged an hour later, well fed and tanked up with tea. Our ravenous appetites had been satisfied, so all we had to do now was decide what we were going to do for the rest of the day. Then of course we would have to start thinking about where we were going to sleep that night. The decision was simultaneous, instantaneous and unanimous. No one needed to say anything; our eyes said it all. In silent but contented exhaustion we walked across the road to the bus station, got on the next bus for Birkenhead and set off on our way home.

Looking back on it later, we all agreed that it was a wonderful experience. We had all thoroughly enjoyed every marrow-chilling minute of it and would not have missed it for all the tea in China. So I wonder why we never did it again.

18

Recipe for Disaster

Afew miles further down the road from Mold, nestling in the Welsh hills, is a place called Colomendy. This is a camp consisting of military-style wooden huts where, in the fifties, Liverpool Education Authority organised summer camps, mainly for the pupils of Liverpool and Cologne, but a few Dutch and Swedish students also found their way there.

Whoever thought up this experiment was a very brave man. The war was still very fresh in the minds of a lot of people and the residents of Liverpool still had vivid memories of the bombing raids (or the 'Blitz', as they were collectively known), the telegrams bringing news of loved ones who had been killed and all the other nightmare events that cause the heartache of war. For many of the older generation the First World War was still a vivid memory, both for those who had returned from the trenches, scarred but alive, and for those whose brothers, sons, husbands and sweethearts had not. So finding it within their hearts to forgive the Germans for what they had inflicted on them in the more recent conflict was not very high on most people's list of priorities. There were few who had not had to cope with personal grief, everyone still remembered the food rationing and coal shortages and there were many still striving to rebuild their lives, shattered by five years of war. Careers had been destroyed, opportunities had been lost and futures thwarted by Hitler's maniacal land-grab ambitions and consuming paranoia. And for many the oft-repeated refrain 'The only good German is a dead German' expressed a sentiment with which they wholeheartedly concurred.

If the emotional damage was still far from being healed the architectural damage to the environment was also a constant, ever-present reminder of the horrors of war. Attempts to come to terms with what history had meted out to the war generation must have been well-nigh impossible when all around people could see vivid reminders of what they had endured. The crippled buildings echoed the crippled minds and bodies trying to cope with the dreadful aftermath of recent events.

Even by the late fifties vast areas of Liverpool had not been rebuilt, and kids would still scamper over the bomb sites and makes dens in the old air-raid shelters as they sang 'Colonel Bogey' and other rude ditties about Hitler and the Nazis. The games they played often involved re-enactments of Second World War battles they had heard about from their dads or seen recalled on the Pathé News 'with Lionel Gamlin reporting' at the Walton Vale or the Palace. No, the war was not forgotten; not by a long chalk.

So the idea of bringing together the kids of Cologne and Liverpool in the late fifties must have seemed just a little premature to many people. And Nan and Mum were among them.

I came home from school one day early in 1959 and told everyone about this summer camp I could go on in North Wales. The cost was minimal, but then the conditions were going to be a touch on the Spartan side, and so the money did not seem to give Mum and Dad too much of a problem. But then I added the rider: 'and we have to agree to bring a couple of Germans home one day for a meal and to meet the family'.

Talk about a deathly hush! It was as if my words had frozen in mid-air. Neither Mum, Dad nor Nan said a word. The only expression on their faces was a total absence of any expression at all. Then Mum and Nan suddenly gulped as a look of horror mixed with total disbelief that I could even suggest such a meeting flashed over their faces. Both went to say something but Nan got in first:

'There'll be nay Gerrrmans in this hoose! I'll swing for the firrrst one who comes through the door!'

Her reaction was understandable. She was one of those people for whom two wars against Germany in a single lifetime were just too much. She lost two brothers in the trenches in the First World War and had agonised for five years over the fate of her two sons when they were away fighting for king and country in the Second. She also had a sister still living in Edinburgh who had suffered permanent mental scarring after losing her fiancé to a German sniper in 1915. So, all in all, it was not surprising that she was less than cock-a-hoop at the thought of having to welcome Jerry into her home. And Mum probably was about to express similar sentiments but Dad did not give her a chance. As someone who had toyed with the idea of becoming a Conchie (Conscientious Objector) in 1939, he had strong views on war and humanity's need to see sense. So when he spoke, he spoke from the heart and was not going to be swayed by Mum and Nan and what he saw as their pointless intransigence.

'Listen, the war's over. This is a new generation. If we can't put the past behind us and start rebuilding the world we'll never stop having wars. If he wants to bring a couple of Germans home he can. Most of them didn't want a war any more than we did.'

And that was that. Dad was not the kind of man to lay down the law all that often, but when he did nobody protested. The very infrequency of his moments of obstinacy lent them a power which it was hopeless to resist. And this was one of those occasions.

I think it was during the second week at Colomendy that we took our guests home. I had become quite friendly with two German lads, Detlef and Heinz, both from the same school in Cologne, and I think they were quite pleased when I invited them to spend the day in Grace Road. So on the appointed day, at the appointed hour, we turned up on the doorstep ready to enjoy some of Mum's home cooking.

Now I knew that Mum was not the world's greatest when it came to getting ready on time. No doubt she had spent all morning cooking, having a fag, wondering what to put on, having another fag, then a cup of tea before nipping round the corner to Oddy's or to the Co-op to buy something she had forgotten. So I gave her plenty of advance warning of when to expect us and told her we would probably turn up at about midday. I also said we would have to have a meal at about one o'clock because we were supposed to show the guests around the neighbourhood before taking them (by bus and ferry) back to Colomendy by about seven. Most of this was perfectly true. The only part of it which was a downright lie was the timing. I knew we would not arrive before one o'clock at the earliest, so I was giving her at least an hour's grace, thinking that even she could get herself ready with that much time to spare. I could not have been more wrong.

Detlef and Heinz were perfect examples of the 'Master Race'. Tall, bronzed and fair-haired, they were dressed immaculately in preparation for meeting my family. I rang the bell. Then my mother appeared and my heart sank. She still had her hair in curlers, which huddled in shame beneath an ancient hair net. A smouldering cigarette dangled lazily from her mouth and, worst of all, her stockings flopped limply around her ankles. And all this was topped with a food-stained, threadbare overall that a guy on Bonfire Night would not have been seen dead in. Would it be an exaggeration to say that I just wanted to curl up and die? No, it would not.

'Oh,' she said, covering her embarrassment with a pitiful attempt at a girlish giggle, 'I didn't think you'd get here so early. Come on in and make yourselves at home.'

Standing in the hall, I introduced the guests. With typical Teutonic correctness they shook hands with Mum, then with Dad, gave a slight bow and (believe it or not) clicked their heels. Then we all traipsed into the sitting room where Nan was sitting by the fire. She did not offer her hand. She just mumbled something about how nice it was to meet them and then did not say another word for the rest of their visit. Occasionally, when I could summon up the courage, I would look at her out of the corner of my eye and see her glowering at the poor lads. The expression 'if looks could kill' springs to mind here.

But the day was not a total failure. Mum produced a superb meal, as she could do (although I had asked her in advance not to cook any cabbage!), which was rounded off with a choice between her wonderful apple pie and her delicious trifle. The apple pie was probably not all that much of a novelty for Heinz and Detlef because of its similarity to their *Apfelstrudel*, but the trifle! That was an unqualified success. It was a delicacy they had never come across before and they polished off the lot. Then, just to complete the experience, they insisted I wrote them out a copy each of the recipe to take home to Germany. This probably saved the day from being an unmitigated disaster. And a year or so later Dad, recalling for some reason what he referred to as the 'German invasion', let his sardonic sense of humour get the better of him. Taking the fag out of his mouth, he chuckled and said, 'The trifle was your Mum's contribution to international understanding and peace in Europe. After all, we haven't had a war with Germany since those lads took her recipe back to the Fatherland, have we?'

The episode with the trifle, it is fair to say, did go some way to breaking the ice a little. All through the meal the conversation had been polite but hardly warm or friendly. Even Dad, whose insistence had made the whole event possible, found it very difficult to forgive and forget when he came face to face with real, live representatives of the nation that such a short time before had been his enemy. And there is a historical irony here. As an RAF instrument mechanic, Dad might well have serviced some of the Lancasters that flew off to bomb Detlef's and Heinz's parents out of their homes in Cologne during the war.

But today he was playing host to their sons.

19

Welsh Rarebit

By and large the simmering animosity shown to Detlef and Heinz during their visit was not reflected in Colomendy. There was the occasional remark passed about the 'Krauts' and when it was discovered that one of the teachers accompanying the Cologne group had been a Wehrmacht paratrooper the temptation was too much for some of the Liverpool lads. On at least two occasions I saw several of them being admonished for goose-stepping when they saw this teacher approaching. And then, one day, somebody shouted '*Heil Hitler!*' at him; that was the last straw. Rumour had it that the lad in question was told in no uncertain terms to pack his bags and was then escorted to the bus stop and told to make his own way home.

These incidents aside, we all got on very well. We played games, organised sporting competitions, went on day trips and held organised concerts and sing-songs in the evenings. All in all it was good-natured, healthy 'Scouting-for-boys'-type fun.

I remember two of the most enthusiastic lads from our group in these activities were a certain Pete Best (the same Pete Best, I think, who later became the Beatles' drummer before Ringo's accession to the position), and Mike McCartney, brother of Sir Paul and member of the group known as The Scaffold.

But much of the time we were allowed to wander off on our own. There was no compulsion to enter into the group activities if you didn't want to. If you wanted to cherry-pick nobody objected, and I certainly took advantage of this freedom. After all, there's only so much camaraderie and bonhomie a body can stand.

So on the middle Saturday afternoon I and another camper (Dave something or other, from a school the other side of Liverpool) decided to stride out on our own and climb the hill near the camp called Moel Fammau. It was not a particularly arduous climb as the gradient is reasonably gentle. The weather was glorious and, after walking along the path leading to the summit for an hour or so we decided to sit down, open our bottles of lemonade and admire the view. The fact that we had both spotted a couple of girls sitting on the grass a few yards further ahead just might have influenced our decision to take a rest at that particular moment in that particular spot. But we, Liverpudlian sophisticates that we were, did not want to make it too obvious that we had seen them.

'I don't like the one you're havin',' Dave whispered in my ear; he had obviously taken a fancy to the blonde.

'You took the words right out of my mouth,' I replied. But I had seen the one sitting on the left with the thickest, darkest hair I had ever seen.

So, pretending not to notice them, we sat down and acted as if we were looking out over the undulating hills into the far distance. Within minutes the girls made some comment about our Liverpool accents and started laughing. We turned. We spoke to them and the deed was done. We had connected. So we got up and moved up right next to them. Before I knew it I had asked the dark haired one for a date.

Now in my rather limited experience of asking girls for a date there were usually three possible replies: 'Yes', 'I'll think about it' and 'Get lost, shorty.'

But this girl won hands down for originality when she replied, 'I might come out with you, but only if you can say "LLANFAIRPWLLGWYNGYLLGOGERYCH-WYRNDROBWLLLLANTYSILIOGOGOGOCH".'

It will probably come as no surprise to hear that I hadn't got a clue what she was talking about. I had heard that somewhere in darkest Wales there was a little village with a name containing 58 letters that was supposed to be the longest place-name in Britain. But pronounce it? I had no idea where to even begin.

I thought that that was it. I failed the 'shibboleth' test miserably and so there was no possibility later on of a kiss and a cuddle with this little Blodwen.

'Oh, well,' she suddenly said, 'I'll give you a second chance. If you let me teach you, I might let you take me out tonight.'

The Welsh railway station on Anglesey with its famous tongue-twister name which few Englishmen (and not all Welshmen!) can pronounce. It's easy to see why it is usually just referred to as Llanfair PG. *(Sutton Collection)*

So she started, and her pedagogical skills were impressive. She split the word up into syllables and made me repeat each one separately before joining them all together. Then, when she thought I had got the hang of it, she made me repeat the whole thing several times before I was able to say it without any prompting in one stupendous, virtuoso solo performance as a grand finale.

'Very good,' she said. 'All right, I can meet you at seven if you like. Can you come into Mold?'

Could I? Does the sun come up every morning? Do the stars twinkle at night?

Dave meanwhile had been working his magic on the other girl. He had got her to agree to a date as well, but I never asked him the details. I had got Diane (the same Diane who explained the meaning of the word 'miscarriage' eighteen months later) to agree to meet me, and that was all I was interested in.

It was now late afternoon and time to go. The four of us made our way back down to the little tea shop by the bus stop. A cup of tea and a cream cake later Dave and I watched as the girls got on to the bus and waved us goodbye. Diane looked at me and drew a figure 7 in the air. I was over the moon.

I got off the bus in Mold just before seven. There she was. Diane was waiting for me. Well, that was a new experience for a start. The few girls I had dated previously always seemed to think it was somehow a girl's privilege (or, as Dad put it, 'a lady's prerogative') to turn up about twenty minutes late.

In those days a first date more often than not was a rather innocent, sedate affair. First of all we went and sat in a coffee bar and just talked and got to know each other a bit more. It turned out she worked in an electrical shop on the road leading out of Mold past Colomendy and out to Ruthin. She was a couple of months older than I was and lived in a street with what sounded to me like a very strange Welsh name. Then she suddenly asked if I remembered how to pronounce Llanfair . . . etc. . . . etc. and was a little surprised I could still make a reasonable stab at it. So then she told me the Welsh for Mold, '*Yr Wyddgrug*', and laughed as I tried to get my tongue around it.

A few cups of frothy coffee later we decided to go for a walk. It was still light and one of those balmy summer evenings which can so easily come to mind when the forgotten memories of youth are awakened. As we were just walking outside the boundaries of this lovely little market town and about to set off down a country road a car suddenly screeched to a halt, right by my side. An irate, ginger-haired youth got out and started shouting at Diane. I had no idea what was going on but I was about to find out.

Diane suddenly grabbed tight hold of my hand and told this lad to leave her alone. It turned out later that he had been pestering her to go out with him but she was not interested. For the moment, however, things looked as if they could turn nasty.

When he realised he was getting nowhere with Diane he turned on me. He didn't actually hit me, but he was very close to it. Instead, he just came out with a mouthful of foul language and predicted a very unpleasant immediate future for me. Kicking my head in was one of the least painful treats he had in store for me.

'Oh, yes?' I said, with my arms akimbo and in an uncharacteristic display of macho bravado, 'You and whose army?'

Usually I stayed out of fights, but for some reason on this occasion I made up my mind that I was not going to be intimidated. If he was going to beat me up he was going to get a seriously bloody nose in the process. So what followed was an eyeball-to-eyeball confrontation. He blinked first. Then he got back in his car and screeched off into the sunset.

I breathed a silent sigh of relief. It had been a tense moment, but I wanted to milk it for all it was worth. Diane had seen me at my heroic best and I was not going to spoil it by letting her see that underneath I had been scared stiff.

The rest of the date was rather uneventful. We arranged to meet the next day, Sunday, at about one thirty in the afternoon. Then a quick, hesitant kiss and I was on the bus back to Colomendy.

It might have been the height of summer but the next morning I was full of the joys of spring. I must have passed the morning in some sort of love-struck daze. All I could think about was getting the bus into Mold and seeing Diane again. It was one of those cliché times: I was counting the minutes to one o'clock when the bus left the We Three Loggerheads pub for the twenty minute journey into Mold.

I was at the bus stop at ten to one. One o'clock came and there was no bus. Five minutes passed and there was still no sign of it. Then ten minutes, fifteen, twenty; now I was starting to get worried. When I looked at my watch and it said 1.30 I walked over to where the timetable was pinned to a small notice-board and scrutinised it. My heart missed a beat. Yes, according to the time-table a bus did leave the We Three Loggerheads at one o'clock every day . . . except Sunday! There was only a bus about every three or four hours on a Sunday and the next one was not due until three o'clock. What the hell was I to do?

What would any red-blooded lad do? I ran. I did. I thought that I could cover the distance in under an hour and there was just a chance Diane might have waited for me at the place we had arranged for our tryst.

But of course she didn't. I ran, walked, ran a bit more and then walked a bit more until I had covered the four or five miles separating Colomendy from Mold. I was exhausted when I arrived, pouring with sweat and ready to drink the River Alyn dry. But Diane was not there when I arrived. I was well over an hour late, so who could blame her for thinking I was not going to turn up?

But then, all of a sudden, there she was, on the other side of the road. I crossed over and was about to start explaining why I was so late, but she anticipated me.

'I realised there was no bus at one o'clock today after I left you last night,' she said, smiling. 'I thought you wouldn't come. How did you get here?'

'I didn't want you to think I didn't want to see you again,' I stammered through parched lips, 'so I ran . . . all the way.'

Diane just smiled again. By now she realised that I was desperately in need of a sit-down and a drink (or three!) so she took me to a little café to recuperate. What happened next I don't remember but it doesn't matter. The important thing was that I had earned more than just a few Brownie points for making the effort.

The pub between Mold and Ruthin which gave us the expression 'to be at loggerheads'. History has it that in the 1780s a local landowner and vicar constantly argued in this hostelry and the publican, Richard Wilson, tried unsuccessfully to act as mediator. *(By courtesy of Sian Stephens and Keith Wilson, We Three Loggerheads)*

We saw each other every night after that for the rest of my stay in Colomendy. There were long walks, hours spent in a coffee bar on Chester Street, visits to the only cinema in Mold: I can still remember seeing a Danny Kaye film in which he played somebody called Mr Jacobowski. Heaven knows why I remember that! Then the camp was over and it was time for me to return home to Liverpool.

What were we going to do? We wanted to see each other again. But the tyranny of distance was going to make things very difficult. Then we had a brainwave. We would meet every Saturday in Chester. The train service between Liverpool and Chester was very good and I could be there in about an hour and a half or two hours at the most. From Mold there was an even better bus service for Diane to use. So that was agreed and the arrangements worked perfectly.

Most Saturday mornings I would catch the steam train from Central station in Liverpool at about 10 o'clock and we would meet on Chester station a couple of hours later. Then we would perhaps go for a sail on the river, sit and have a picnic on the river bank or, when summer faded into autumn and autumn slid into winter we would go to the pictures or sit in a café making eyes at each other and planning for the future. If one of us for some reason couldn't make it on the Saturday I would usually travel to Mold on the Sunday as the thought of not seeing each other for two weeks was just too much to contemplate. These were the golden, innocent days of youth when every hour spent together was precious and, to borrow John Milton's phrase, 'beyond the bliss of dreams'. We were in love and we swore we would be together for eternity.

But in our case eternity lasted about eighteen months.

20

Glowing Futures

Back home in Liverpool the sixth form beckoned. I had fulfilled my side of the bargain I had entered into with Mr Dunn by passing a few O levels a year early and now he was keeping his. So in September 1959 I became a whole Sixth Form class by myself. I was the only one of my contemporaries who wanted to study languages and so I became L6ML (Lower Sixth Modern Languages), taking English, French and Spanish to A level at the same time as continuing with O level maths. I also began a two-year course leading to an O level in Latin.

And they were carefree days. Yes, there was a lot of work to do, but at least I was now studying mainly subjects I was interested in. There was a pleasant atmosphere in the school and, as sixth-formers, we were treated by the staff as young adults rather than pestilential kids.

Outside school this was the era of the coffee bar and one of the biggest in Liverpool, the El Cabala, opened in Bold Street. It became a popular haunt for all types. There were the pseudo-intellectuals from the university who smoked their pipes, drank coffee and attempted to sound intelligent by discussing Sartre, Proust, Marx, Existentialism, Communism, the imminent fall of Capitalism and religion and so on. Then there were the young banker types whose only topic of conversation was the ups and downs of the stock market and their unshakable conviction that the sixties were going to be the boom years. In a sense they were not a million miles off course, as we were on the threshold of the Macmillan era of 'you've never had it so good'. Consumer goods which the previous generation could only dream about (cars, fridges, washing machines) were about to fall within the reach of most households. The good times were coming and they wanted their share of it.

The third group of El Cabala habitués were the Bold Street shop girls. Now these girls thought of themselves as being a cut above the others who worked in places such as Hendersons and Marks & Spencers or the Co-op. These were the *crème de la crème* who spoke in a sort of posh Scouse accent and referred to dresses as gowns and always sat near the window of the El Cabala, daintily fingering their long cigarettes as they wittered on about the price of nylons, the latest fashions or the newest shoe shop which had just opened in the town.

A busy scene in Church Street in the 1930s. (*Sutton Collection*)

I fell into yet another group. We were too young (not to mention ignorant!) to fit in with the undergraduate types and far too poor to be acceptable to the thrusting young businessmen. And for the refined ladies from the neighbouring gown shops we did not even exist. No, we were the tolerated ones. We were still at school and dependent on the £1 a week pocket money we got from our parents to fund our social life, so the high life had to wait. We were past masters at making a cup of coffee last for a whole hour.

For a change we would sometimes meet in the Kardomah on Church Street. The Kardomah had an atmosphere and a feel about it that was all its own. There was none of the spindly furniture which characterised the El Cabala ('contemporary design', as it was known) and which had been creeping into shops, cafés and even homes everywhere since the mid-fifties. Oh no; the Kardomah clung on to its solid mahogany tables and chairs which symbolised a permanence that flew in the face of the spirit of the age. The emphasis now was on the flimsy, the transient and the disposable, and it was probably this very air of solidity which contributed to the Kardomah's demise. In an increasingly throw-away society people wanted chip-board and plywood tat, and they just turned away from mahogany and oak.

The waitresses in these establishments were special too. They all wore old-fashioned black dresses and beautifully starched white aprons and little caps so that they looked like the 'nippies' in the pre-war 'Lyons tea-shops'. In fact, there was a generally anachronistic atmosphere about the Kardomah which was part, if not all, of its charm.

Then there was the aroma of real, beautiful coffee that coaxed passers-by to step inside and sample the delights on offer. The Kardomah was less artificial, less showy and simply more inviting than the pretentious El Cabala.

It was over a cup of coffee in the Kardomah one Saturday morning that Pete Kvalen dropped his bombshell.

Of all the pupils in Hillfoot Pete was probably the brightest. He was good at maths, physics and chemistry but was also within striking distance of being 'top of the form' in arts subjects as well. Spanish was the only subject I could beat him at in the exams and that was never by anything more than a couple of marks. If anyone was destined for a brilliant university career he was.

He was also extremely shy. When most of us were chasing the girls and had discovered pubs Pete never joined in. If a girl just said 'hello' to him in the street he would blush to the roots of his hair. And as for joining us for a night out in Liverpool for a few drinks in the pub, he just was not interested.

So it came as a shock when he suddenly announced that he was fed up with school, had decided to leave and had already got himself fixed up with a job as a trainee clerk in the Gas Board.

But he soon gave us all another shock. The Gas Board didn't turn out to be all he had hoped it would be. Pete had just finished a couple of weeks of mind-numbing pen-pushing behind a Gas Board desk when we bumped into each other in town one afternoon. He magnanimously said he would let me buy him a coffee and as we were making our way to our favourite coffee shop he announced in a matter-of-fact manner, 'Don't like working. I've jacked it in. I'm going round the world.'

'Oh,' I said. 'That sounds interesting. Have you won the pools? Going on a cruise, then?'

'No,' he replied with a steely ring of determination in his voice. 'I'm just going to set off and hitch-hike my way around.'

I could not believe my ears. Stay-at-home Pete had decided to go hitch-hiking around the world? Never!

'I've got it all planned out. I'm setting off next Friday and first of all I'm going to make my way down to the south coast and get across into France. Then through Spain and into North Africa. Then I'm just going to play it by ear.'

'I bet you turn back before you've even got to London,' I said in my usual supportive manner.

'You're on. I'll send you a postcard from Hong Kong!'

He did not send me the card. At least not from Hong Kong. But I did get a card from him from San Francisco the better part of a year later. He had done it. Confounding all the sceptics (I was not the only one who thought he would fail), he made his way through Europe, crossed into Turkey and then somehow through parts of Asia, crossed the Pacific and ended up on the west coast of America.

When I saw him next, about two years after our conversation on our way down to the Kardomah, he was a changed man. And that's the operative word: man. The shy teenager who set off on his own with little more to guide him but a romantic dream had returned a confident, experienced explorer who had literally had the whole world at his feet and was now ready to carve out a future for himself. And he did. But not in Liverpool. He had tasted foreign fare and wanted more of it. So, after a brief stay at home he packed his bags again and set off for San Francisco once more. And the last time I heard from him he was still there.

The coffee-bar culture flourished in Liverpool in those days, as it did in the rest of the country. It was symbolic of the growing affluence the younger generation were starting to enjoy, much to the annoyance of some of the older folk. Restaurants seemed to breed all over the place and very ordinary people were now sampling the pleasures which before the war had been the preserve of the well-off few. But the prices were sky-high. A meal for two at a reasonable restaurant such as Sampson and Barlow's on London Road would consist of prawn cocktail, T-bone steak followed by a slice of Black Forest gateau and a cup of tea (wine was still almost unknown) and would leave little change out of a fiver. In those days this could be almost a week's wage. And certainly, many of our parents' generation found it difficult to understand how the teenagers could spend in an evening more than what most mothers had to feed families on for a week.

In a sense Pete Kvalen and the El Cabala summed up the spirit of the age. The Kardomah was rooted in the past; the El Cabala hailed the brave new world of youth and optimism for the future. Pete represented the new determination to get out and see the world. Package tours to Spain made foreign travel accessible to almost all, so that the pre-war week's holiday in Blackpool or Llandudno was no longer enough. Horizons broadened and the 1960s were going to be for the generation who wanted to get out and do things and leave their parents at home by the fireside with their fading memories of unemployment in the 1930s and the war against Hitler in the forties.

The only cloud on the skyline was ominously mushroom-shaped. From as far back as the late forties people had been learning to live with the threat of nuclear war. But although it was always in the back of our minds it did not stop us getting on with our lives. A certain fatalism crept into the collective psyche and we saw no point in worrying about the next world war; if and when it came it would be nuclear and the obliteration would be total. The newspapers of the day left readers in no doubt about the horrors we might expect, particularly when the atom bombs of Hiroshima and Nagasaki were superseded by the far more powerful and more destructive hydrogen bomb. The pithy saying at the time summed up our resignation: 'There's only one thing worse than dying in a nuclear war and that's *not* dying in a nuclear war.' So we were faced with two possibilities: an affluent future, fuelled by burgeoning consumerism, or Armageddon. The vast majority of us just fixed our gaze on the former and closed our eyes to the latter.

21

The Brush-off

A few minutes' walk from Castle Street and the commercial centre of Liverpool there was another world. All any stranger to the city had to do before the slum clearances of the 1960s was seek out the narrow lanes in the shadows of the magnificent architecture and he would come face to face with a grimmer side of the city's history. Behind the majestic edifices erected at the height of Liverpool's mercantile glory stood the other, meaner buildings on which the wealth of the city depended. Here the narrow alleyways, tiny houses and filthy courtyards told of a way of life for their inhabitants that was very different from that suggested by the buildings modelled on the temples of ancient Greece and Rome. St George's Hall, the Picton and William Brown libraries and the Walker Art Gallery might impress the visitor with their classical splendour, but they also hid an unpalatable truth which few of those in authority wished to admit: the vast riches that flooded into the city in its heyday were enjoyed by few of those whose sweat created it. The imposing Town Hall might symbolise nineteenth-century affluence but it turned its back, literally and metaphorically, on the squalid homes of Liverpool's working men. And this same Town Hall rarely acknowledged the sweated labour that paid for its own grand façade.

But the Town Hall has other historical associations of which it should be less than proud. Every day hundreds, if not thousands, of people rush past this beautiful building and never notice the figures etched into its walls. If they stopped for a moment and examined the carvings there they would see lions, elephants, crocodiles and human beings of distinctly African appearance, all frozen in time and symbolising the link between Liverpool and Africa. The reason for these unlikely decorations is summed up in one shameful word: slavery. The sad but inescapable truth is that much of the wealth of the city was amassed in the eighteenth century by Liverpool merchants whose involvement in the slave trade was never less than enthusiastic. And their occupation apparently never caused them so much as even a twinge of conscience. Far from skulking away or hiding the extent of their involvement in the dreadful business, they advertised it by including symbolic carvings of their commerce in the buildings they erected with the profits or which at least had dealings with the trade. And woe betide anyone who dared to suggest that what they did was unethical. There is a story of one visitor to the town who was almost lynched by an angry mob because he had the gall to suggest that every building in Liverpool had been 'cemented with the blood of an African'.

The business centre of Liverpool, Castle Street, with the Town Hall in the background. *(Sutton Collection)*

We can now shake our heads in disbelief that so much of the nation's wealth was gained through slavery, but we cannot change history. What's done is done. Liverpool was the principal port in what was known as the Trade Triangle. Slave ships would leave Liverpool and sail to the west coast of Africa where they would pick up their human cargoes. Men, women and children were then transported in unspeakably inhumane conditions across the Atlantic to the Americas, where they were handed over into slavery in exchange for commodities such as cotton, rum, tobacco and coffee, which were then brought back and unloaded in Liverpool.

One of the little side-streets near this part of the city takes the first-time visitor back in time and introduces him to the warehouses and grain-stores where the toilers of an earlier age slogged their guts out from dawn until dusk, working up a God-almighty thirst which they then slaked in one of the nearby spit-and-sawdust pubs. And one of these buildings, a nondescript, unprepossessing former warehouse used for storing fruit as it awaited transport to market, was to achieve worldwide fame as a venue for the young men of Liverpool who changed the face of popular entertainment the world over. The street is Mathew Street and the warehouse is now known to all as The Cavern.

Hardly anybody outside Liverpool had heard of the Cavern before the sixties, and in most people's minds it is still associated with the Beatles. The truth is, however, that it had been in existence since 1957 as a jazz cellar and groups such as the Quarrymen (who transmogrified into the Beatles), Gerry and the Pacemakers, The Merseybeats and dozens more were the Johnnies-come-lately who benefited from the success of jazz performers such as The Merseysippi Jazz Band, Acker Bilk and his Paramount Jazz Band, and George Melly.

The Cavern in those days was potentially a very dangerous place to be. It was a cellar consisting of three long arched vaults and the only way in (or out!) was by a wooden staircase. I dread to think what would have happened had there been a fire, but in those days, before the health and safety culture got a grip, we did not think of such things.

Liverpool's magnificent St George's Hall, designed by the architect Harvey Lonsdale Elmes when he was only twenty-five. The influence of Classical Greek architecture in general and the Parthenon in Athens in particular is obvious. *(Catherine Rothwell)*

The Walker Art Gallery, another superb building in the Classical (Corinthian) style. *(Catherine Rothwell)*

The Picton Library, also adorned with Corinthian pillars, was opened in 1879. Locally it is referred to as 'Picton's Gasometer'. *(Catherine Rothwell)*

The lighting was very bad, in fact almost non-existent. The stage and performers were well lit, but there was hardly any lighting for the audience, who sat or stood in the permanent penumbra cast on to them from the stage. No alcohol was sold in the early days, but almost everybody smoked, so the potential for a serious accident was always there.

It was George Melly, also a native Scouser, who was the star attraction on the night of my first visit to the cavern in 1958 or 1959. And 'star' is the only word to describe him. He was the consummate artist whose professionalism and sheer talent, to my mind, put everyone else in the shade. His performance that night of 'Hard-hearted Hannah, the vamp of Savannah' was unbelievable and without doubt one of the most memorable acts by a singer I have ever seen.

Even the Beatles and their ilk, despite all their fame and fortune, never matched the originality, brilliance and sheer genius of George at his performing best. But jazz had had its day. For a brief period skiffle (jazz improvised on household implements) had a moment of glory, but then came the beat groups who, by the early

Another great building, the Brown Library, named after Sir William Brown MP, stands next door to the Picton. It was opened in 1860. *(Catherine Rothwell)*

sixties, had taken the world by storm. As in so many other walks of life in those days, it was a case of 'out with the old and in with the new'. So the new boys took over.

Many of the older, die-hard jazz fans found that they could not adjust. They simply did not like the new music or the groups that produced it, and that was all there was to it. With one or two notable exceptions most of the new boys were talentless in the extreme. Few of them could sing and many knew absolutely nothing about music. They had just learned to play a few chords in the kitchen of their two-up and two-downs and repeated them mercilessly on their guitars. They could make a lot of noise, but much of it was appallingly tuneless and some groups, if the truth be told, even if they had practised day and night for a century, would have had a tough job reaching mediocre. The skilled musicianship of the old jazz bands was no longer a requirement.

But for the less discerning, like myself, the change was no real problem. It didn't prevent me or any of my friends from making the Cavern a favourite haunt on a Friday night. At first a group of us from Aintree used to catch the bus into the city centre and head straight for the dingy cellar we all came to know and love. But after a while we discovered how we could pad out an evening by paying a visit to one of Liverpool's myriad hostelries before wending our somewhat unsteady way to the teetotal Cavern. Frequently an evening's entertainment was initiated with the trad-itional Scouse invitation: 'Are yiz cumin down de pier 'ead for a bevy?' In standard

English, this is a suggestion to visit the Pier Head and partake of an alcoholic libation.

So the pattern was established: a few pints at the Pier Head, a walk up Water Street, a right turn into North John Street and then a left turn into Mathew Street. Not infrequently there would be a quick visit to the Grapes, right opposite the Cavern, and no doubt another pint or two before we crossed the road to listen to some group's abysmal attempt at singing in tune.

Descending the wooden stair into the basement was like entering another world where the sweaty denizens of this stifling, smoky, subterranean lair seemed totally isolated from life outside. Some would dance enthusiastically to the beat of the deafening music near the stage while others smooched passionately in the darkest corners. But many of the girls were 'groupies', only interested in catching Ringo's, Paul's, John's or George's eye, and they, in an almost apoplectic frenzy,

Interior of the Cavern. Note how most of the audience seems singularly unimpressed with the performance on stage. (*Liverpool Record Office*)

would congregate as close to the stage as they could, reaching out and trying to touch whichever teen idol was standing closest to them at the time. But the stories of their taking off items of underwear and throwing them at John Lennon or Gerry Marsden are probably apocryphal; at least, I never saw it happen on any of my visits.

On one of my last visits to the Cavern, sometime around the autumn or winter of 1961, I noticed there was a new girl in the cloakroom, taking the coats off people as they came in, handing them a cloakroom ticket and then reversing the process as they left. She had shiny, dark hair which seemed to cling to her oval face, and her smile could have charmed the hardest of hearts. Her shining eyes and ready laughter completed the delightful picture.

'I haven't seen you here before,' I said. 'Been working here long?'

It was not a very original chat-up line, but it was the best I could think of at the moment.

'Not long,' she replied, a little frostily.

'What's your name, then?' I asked.

'Miss White to you,' she replied as her winning smile deserted her face and the initial frostiness turned to rock-hard ice.

My courage evaporated. I didn't bother attempting to take the conversation any further as it was obviously going nowhere. So I just handed over my coat, picked up my cloakroom ticket and made my way through the heaving throng to where my friends were already standing. My pitiful attempt at chatting the girl up had been witnessed by most of the gang and so I became the butt of their jokes for the rest of the evening.

'Her name's Priscilla,' someone said later on. 'I know 'cos a friend of mine's been out with 'er.'

As the evening wore on I could see Priscilla, who was now standing to the left of the stage watching the show, and that same voice that had once dared me to go into a pub for the first time and order a pint started talking to me again. 'Go on,' it said, 'have another go. What are you, man or mouse? She can only say no.'

So I girded my loins and headed straight for her. I was in a resolute mood when I started to plough my way through the dense crowd of perspiring humanity, but by the time I was within talking distance most of my courage had subsided. An adolescent timidity seemed to grip me by the throat and the self-assured confidence I wanted to display just left me high and dry.

'I've . . . got some tickets for . . . a school dance next week. Do you . . . fancy coming with me?' I asked, hesitantly.

'Sorry la',' she said in her Scottie (Scouse for Scotland) Road accent. 'I've already gorra boy friend so de answer's no.'

So that was that. She had brushed me aside twice and there was no way I was going to give her a chance to do it for a third time. After all, I had my pride. And the two phrases we always uttered inwardly for consolation when we found ourselves in that situation flashed across my mind in rapid succession: 'There's plenty more fish in the sea' and 'She's not the only pebble on the beach.'

The run-down, dismal exterior of the Cavern as it was in the 1950s and '60s. *(Liverpool Record Office)*

But I did see her again, a year or two later. We were all sitting round the fire at home watching the telly and I seem to remember *Sunday Night at the London Palladium*, hosted by Bruce Forsyth, when all of a sudden there she was on the screen in our front room. There was no doubt about it. I'd recognise that smile anywhere. It was Priscilla, the girl who had given me the brush-off and turned down my offer of a wonderful night out at a Hillfoot Hey school dance. Now she was a world-famous super-star for whom my chat-up lines would not even be a distant, fuzzy memory.

But Miss Priscilla White had changed her name to Cilla Black. Just think what she missed and how different her life might have been if she had accepted my offer! But she had her chance and she blew it.

22

Status

There was something schizophrenic about the sixth form. The A level languages exams in those days were heavily biased towards literature and so from Monday to Friday (and part of the weekend as well) I found myself immersed in the works of French, Spanish and English authors. This meant that most of my waking hours were spent reading Molière, Racine, Cervantes, Shakespeare and other classical writers too numerous to mention. The upshot was that for much of the time my thoughts, my imagination and my critical faculties were more concerned with the events and problems affecting fictional characters inhabiting a world that had disappeared centuries earlier. Inevitably I was enmeshed in an escapist fantasy world for much of the week. At 9.30 in Mr Finney's English literature class I could be a Roman soldier in Egypt as I found myself reading the part of Enobarbus in *Antony and Cleopatra* or I was convinced I was Angel Clare as we read a chapter from *Tess of the D'Urbervilles*. An hour later I might be climbing into the skin of a character out of a seventeenth-century French farce or suffering delusions of grandeur along with Don Quixote in sixteenth-century Spain. Then I would suddenly find myself back in the twentieth century when the bell rang at about four o'clock to announce the end of the school day.

Life at home could be similarly schizophrenic. On the one hand, Dad was pleased to know that I was studying classical authors as, in his youth, he had been an avid reader of Dickens, Hardy and the other greats of English literature. But Mum was at the other end of the spectrum: I never saw her read anything other than the odd article in a women's magazine. And the mere suggestion that she should even contemplate reading one of the classics would have been met with a firm rebuff if not scathing derision. She had come to terms, albeit reluctantly, with my not studying to be a doctor and just about accepted that languages could be a worthwhile study. But why did I have to study so much literature? What was the point of that? When I mentioned the value of art for art's sake and then came out with words such as 'culture' or 'intellectual' she would wince visibly. One Sunday morning when I bought the *Sunday Times* because of an article they were running that week on contemporary French writers she just did not know how to cope. She was desperate for me to get into university (just think of the social kudos attached to having a son at university!) but could not understand why I was so interested in airy-fairy subjects like literature. The idea of going out specially to buy an extra newspaper just because of an article on a bunch of froggie scribblers was totally beyond her understanding. We already had the *News of the World*, the *Sunday Post* and another paper with the magnificently anachronistic, non-PC-sounding title the *Empire News* delivered every Sunday morning. So what was so special about the *Sunday Times*, apart from the fact that nobody else in the house would want to read it? After all, Sunday papers were for sport, juicy scandal and horoscopes, weren't they?

Then when the French master, Harry Green, started trying to make me understand that there was a link between literature and philosophy she just gave up. If I tried to turn the usual teatime conversations away from football, horse-racing, the price of carrots at the Nutshell or boiled ham at the Home and Colonial and discuss the real purpose of literature, the nature of art or the definition of words such as 'good' and 'evil' she would light a fag and immediately start washing the dishes. With that job out of the way she would then turn the telly on to watch *Coronation Street*, the new twice-weekly programme everyone was talking about. Forget *The Odyssey* and *The Iliad*: *Coronation Street* was the new epic of twentieth-century oral literature.

But her attitude to reading was not consistent. Before I acquired the habit of losing myself in some gripping yarn she was forever reminding me of the benefits of reading. She was always telling me how it would help with my spelling and help develop my powers of expression as well as increase my general knowledge. The educational advantages of the reading were limitless. Or so she kept saying.

So why did she have the opposite attitude with my sister? Marg had been a voracious reader from early childhood and could disappear to her bedroom for hours on end and lose herself completely in *Wuthering Heights*, *Gone with the Wind* or any of the other dozen or so books she would come back from the library with once or twice a week. As far as Mum was concerned girls should not be wasting their time reading (or, as she usually expressed it, with their 'heads stuck in a book'), as education was somehow not something that should concern girls. The result was that sometimes within the space of no more than a few minutes I could be getting an ear-bashing from Mum for not reading enough and Marg would be similarly reprimanded for reading too much!

But Mum probably had this dual attitude to the value of the written word because of the times she herself grew up in. And even as late as the fifties and sixties there were still many adults who thought that education (and certainly further education) was only for the boys. After all, they were the future bread-winners who would be able to get a better-paid (and, just as important, a higher-status) job if they had a good education. For her generation a grammar-school education was a dream beyond the reach of many. And of those working-class children who were bright enough to pass the exam to get into a grammar school many had to forgo the opportunity because their parents could not afford the money to buy the uniform and textbooks. Then there were the families where perhaps a brother and sister were both intelligent enough to be offered grammar-school places but the parents could only afford to pay for one child to accept the offer. And inevitably it was the boy who would be favoured. Girls, after all, were just marriage-fodder for whom a Leaving Certificate pass in Latin, French or maths was useless: you don't need to be able to conjugate Latin verbs in order to change babies' nappies.

Although the situation had changed dramatically by the 1950s so that there was free secondary and tertiary education for anyone who could pass the required examinations, the attitudes of the older generation were slow to change. And the school curriculum frequently reflected this difference of attitude towards boys and girls. The girls spent a lot of their day learning how to cook, wash clothes, sew, darn and do the ironing. Nobody ever doubted that the vast majority of them would end up as domestic goddesses.

But it was expected that a girl would work for a few years before settling down into the role predetermined for her by Mother Nature. And social attitudes came into play here as well. If a girl left school with sufficient expertise in shorthand and typing she would have a good chance of landing herself a job in an office. In the scheme of things a position as a secretary was considered a cut above a job as a shop assistant or factory girl. Hartleys jam factory, Jacobs biscuit factory and Lucas's car components factory were probably among the biggest employers in Aintree in the fifties and sixties, and to get job with one of these firms offered a stability and security which the previous generation had never known. But from a sociological point of view a lot depended on which part of the factory you worked in. Office workers, secretaries, book-keepers and so on ('white-collar workers') were certainly considered a step up the social ladder from the school-leavers whose lack of qualifications meant that they could only find employment on the factory floor, along with the other 'blue-collar workers'.

So when Marg announced to all the world that she wanted to be a children's nurse, Mum's somewhat peculiar, not to mention eccentric, concept of democratic choice and the freedom of the individual made itself evident yet again.

'You can forget that right away,' she said, having given the matter her full and undivided attention and considered my sister's wishes and inclinations for at least a second and a half, 'and you can find yourself a job in an office.'

'But Ann Kelly doesn't work in an office. She works in a shop,' Marg answered.

Ann Kelly was my sister's best friend, and she and Mum always got on very well together, probably because of the naturally refined 'lady-like' way Ann had of speaking and behaving.

'That's different,' Mum continued. 'She's a trained florist. It's not the same thing at all. You can find yourself a job in an office, and that's all there is to it. You meet a better class of people in offices.'

But when my sister failed to show any enthusiasm for the life of an office girl and consequently did little about finding secretarial work, Mum took matters into her own hands. The family doctor, Dr Bannerman, had some family or professional connection with the personnel department at the Jacobs biscuit factory on Long Lane and so he was dragooned in to help. Now Mum was nothing if not a very persuasive lady and so, within a very short period of time, the good doctor had pulled a few strings and – lo and behold! – Marg was employed by Jacobs as a shorthand typist.

Mum was pleased with the outcome. She could now hold her head up high when talking to the neighbours; Marg had found employment in a socially more acceptable position.

I wonder if this view of the world had anything to do with the fact that Mum was an office manager.

23

Union Jack

The phone rang. Mum went to answer it. She didn't say very much, just 'Yes . . . I see . . . ha . . . aha . . . of course, Mr Dunn . . . all right . . . yes . . . I'll tell him . . . thank you for calling.' 'That was your headmaster,' she said when she came back into the kitchen. 'He's talking about you going to live in France and wanted my ideas about it first before mentioning it to you. Not sure I like the idea, but he wants you to go and see him straight after assembly tomorrow morning.'

The next morning I couldn't wait to find out what Mr Dunn had planned for me and was outside his office within seconds of the morning assembly finishing. What he had in mind was not my going to live in France on a permanent basis but it was the next best thing.

'How would you like to live with a French family for a few weeks? Mr Forbes knows a family just outside Paris and they would be willing to put you up for four or five weeks. They don't speak any English so you would be forced to speak French all the time. Mr Green thinks it would be a good idea, too, especially if we can time it for just before your "A" levels. The local education authority would probably give you a grant. What do you think about the idea?'

By coincidence Mr Finney, only the day before, had been stressing the importance of seizing opportunities when they arise or missing them forever and living to regret it. To back up his argument he had quoted the lines from Shakespeare's *Julius Caesar*:

> There is a tide in the affairs of men
> Which, taken at the flood leads on to fortune;
> Omitted, all the voyage of their life
> Is bound in shallows and in miseries.

This was one tide I just did not want to miss and there was no way I was going to spend the rest of my life 'in shallows and in miseries' if I could help it. Paris? Wow! Please God, don't let Mum say no!

Dad was all for it. He thought it would be a great opportunity for me to go out and see something of the world, as well as a chance to fend for myself and learn some independence. Mum (as ever) had her doubts and misgivings. She did not like the thought of my being so far away and out of her control for so long. I had told her perhaps a little too much about drinking beer and talking (talking!) to French girls on my previous school trip to France so she obviously wondered what I would get up to on my own, off the leash, in the fleshpots of Paris. But she eventually agreed at least to think about it.

For a teenager in those days from a working-class district of Liverpool to get the chance of going abroad to study was not just something of a novelty; it was totally unheard of. Few of the neighbours had ever set foot outside England, apart from the boys who had gone off to fight in 1914 and 1939. For the generations whose experience of travel was limited to a week (or, in many cases, not even that) at some seaside resort no more than a day's train or bus ride away, the chance of travelling to France could only be a pipe-dream. So when they heard of my good fortune their first reaction was one of disbelief. This was Liverpool. We were working class. Money was tight, but here was a local lad who was being paid for to study in Paris.

There were two categories of second reaction. Some of the neighbours, and even one or two relatives, like Uncle Jack, down from Edinburgh on a visit, thought I was being spoiled at the taxpayers' expense and expressed the opinion that it was high time I stopped messing about in school and got out and found a 'proper' job. In his day only the rich could have entertained the idea of a further education, and going abroad to study sounded like the life of Riley. The Welfare State was creating a generation of softies who wanted to waste their time reading and studying instead of getting off their backsides and earning some money. 'It's time you put some bread on the table,' he said one day when he trapped me alone in the kitchen. 'Your Mum and Dad've worked hard all their lives and it's time you started to do the same.'

Other people had a more charitable second reaction. Virtually all of them had had a rough time of it in their youth, but these were the ones who did not begrudge the post-war generation the brighter future it was obviously going to enjoy. And Dad fell into this category.

Now Dad had had an even harder upbringing than Uncle Jack. His father had been a railway shunter, struggling to bring up six or seven children on his own after his wife died just before the First World War. There was hardly enough money to pay for the bare essentials and he, like his brothers and sisters, had had no option but to leave school at the first opportunity and make at least a meagre contribution to the family budget.

By contrast, Jack had had a relatively more affluent upbringing in what was considered to be one of the posher parts of town. Granddad had always had a reasonably good job and money never seems to have been much of a problem. And later on, when they were young men, Jack had never been out of work, not even during the depression of the thirties, but Dad had. He had known the bitter taste of accepting charity and knew what it felt like to sit at a table and enjoy the fruits of other men's labours. He was a proud man, a hard worker (given the chance) and he insisted on paying his way. So when he found himself unemployed periodically and forced to live with his parents-in-law even though he could make no contribution to the family finances it hurt him deeply. But it did not leave him with any feelings of jealousy towards me or any of my friends who were embarking on a life of far greater ease than his generation had known.

So when Dad came into the kitchen and heard Jack upbraiding me for being an idle layabout scared of hard work (he once called me a seg – a northern term for a callus – because, according to him, I only showed up after all the hard work had been done) he got closer to losing his temper than I ever saw him.

'Don't you talk to him like that,' he said. 'If he's bright enough to stay on at school and go to university, good on 'im. I'd 'ave done it if I'd 'ad the chance. It's about time kids in this country 'ad a better chance than we 'ad.'

'I didn't go away and fight a bleedin' war to support kids like 'im who don't know what it's like to do a day's work,' Jack replied, getting on his high horse (Nan's expression).

'Who do you think you're talking to?' Dad came back at him. 'Don't forget I was in the forces too, so you can't tell me what we were fighting for. And I wasn't fighting to come back to the world we left where only rich kids got the chance of a decent education. Things are different now, and a good thing too. If the government wants kids like 'im to continue with their education and is willing to support them financially, that's fine by me.'

I didn't want to get involved in this argument so I excused myself by saying that I had to go to the library to look up a few things for an essay I had to write by Monday. It was a deliberate intellectual stiletto attack and it pierced the very heart of Uncle Jack's prejudices. He winced at the thought of a healthy seventeen-year-old lad still 'wasting time' writing essays at school. As he was quick to point out, many of his comrades at El Alamein and in the Italian campaign had been not much older than seventeen. And a lot of them did not come home.

'All the more reason to educate people and try to make sure it doesn't happen again,' Dad said.

Jack knew he had no answer to that. Dad just smiled at me, said he had something to do and disappeared upstairs.

But I have to admit that I was not too concerned about what people thought. If some thought my going off to spend some time in Paris was a waste of public money that was their problem, not mine. My immediate concern was to persuade Mum to come down off the fence and make a definite decision.

Her problem was not just that she was not particularly enamoured of the idea of my being so far away that she couldn't keep her eye on me. She also had this innate dislike of anything foreign and so the thought of my living in a family of foreigners, speaking a foreign language and eating foreign food was a touch more than she could cope with. She (and she was not alone in her belief) thought that all foreigners should learn English, that England was the finest country in the world and any culinary technique that did not revolve around meat and two veg was barbaric. Then when Marg came in and told her that she and Bill were thinking of having a holiday in Italy at about the same time as I would be in France it was just too much for her.

'Ye Godfathers,' she blurted out (one of her favourite expressions), 'is this country not good enough for anybody any more? Alex wants to go to France and now you say you want to go to Italy. What do you want to go there for? Your Uncle

Jack was in Italy in 1944 and never wants to go back. What's wrong with this country for a holiday? You could just go back to Llandudno.'

'Nineteen forty-four was sixteen years ago! And there was a war on,' said Marg. 'Anyway, it's up to Bill and me where we go on holiday, and we certainly don't want to go to Llandudno! We want to see what it's like abroad.'

'Well,' said Mum, trying the tactics of fear, 'I know someone who went on holiday to Italy last year and she brought her husband home in a box.'

But Marg was having none of this. She just repeated that she was going and there was nothing Mum could do about it. And there wasn't.

Eventually I persuaded her to say yes to my Paris adventure. Once she fully grasped the potential for impressing relatives and neighbours by telling them that I was going off to study abroad she relented. She and Dad went and discussed the details with Mr Dunn, filled out all the paperwork involved with a grant application and then Mum set about finding the cheapest way for me to get to France.

It was Easter 1961 and I was on my way. *Au revoir*, Aintree; *bonjour*, Paris.

24

A la Parisienne

It was raining when I arrived in Ablon-sur-Seine, on the outskirts of Paris. No, it was not just raining, it was pouring down, and when I eventually found the house where I was to spend the next month or so I was soaked to the skin. When Monsieur Dupont opened the front door what he saw in front of him must have looked more like a drowned rat than a member of the human race. But his welcome was warm, as was that of his wife, who came racing out of the kitchen when she realised that the caller was the young Englishman who was going to be their house guest for the next few weeks.

Within about five or ten minutes I realised that this stay was going to do wonders for my French. Neither Monsieur nor Madame spoke any English but they rattled away ten to the dozen in French, both at the same time but asking me different questions so that the effect was like listening to two very different radio programmes simultaneously. I hardly understood either of them as I was exhausted, wet through and freezing, feeling totally miserable and wondering already how I was going to cope. But I needn't have worried.

The welcome, as I say, was warm and as soon as I had been shown my room and changed into some dry clothes I came downstairs again to be met by an enormous drink of what Madame called '*un grog*' which, I soon realised, was very similar to what Nan referred to as 'hot toddy'. It was simply a double shot of whisky mixed with hot water, a spoonful of sugar and a slice of lemon. It tasted wonderful and was just the thing to warm the cockles of my heart and (pardon the pun!) raise my spirits. It also had a wonderfully relaxing effect on my tongue, so that within no more than half an hour I was making my first attempts at engaging in a reasonably coherent conversation with my hosts. I probably sounded dreadful, but I was making an effort and was on my way. Within no time at all, I convinced myself, I would be speaking French like a regular Maurice Chevalier and when I got back home no girl would be able to resist my soon-to-be-acquired Gallic charm.

Dinner was at eight. At half past seven relatives and friends of the Duponts started arriving in what seemed to me like droves. Then we all proceeded into a rather grand dining room and took our places at an enormous oval table which had no difficulty in accommodating the final count of ten or twelve guests.

This was an entirely new experience for me. Family dinners in Grace Road were always a bit of a squeeze, with five or six of us sitting cheek by jowl around the table and such repasts only occurred on Sundays and Christmas Day. During the week we ate on an as-and-when basis in the kitchen but never as a family around the dining-room table. And the usual format for the evening was for us to get it down as fast as we could, then get the dishes washed and out of the way so Mum and Dad could flop in front of the telly, light a fag and watch Hughie Green's *Opportunity Knocks*, Michael Miles's *Take your Pick* or the new police drama *Z Cars*.

In Ablon-sur-Seine things were very different. At first I thought that the meal on the day of my arrival was a sort of welcoming party for their foreign guest, but I was mistaken. Dinner was always the same, every day during my stay. It started promptly at eight, with all the family, that is to say Monsieur et Madame, their thirty-something daughter and her son, a variety of friends and/or neighbours and me. The meal itself always consisted of four or five courses and was accompanied by copious amounts of red wine which, I was informed, served two purposes: it enhanced the flavour of the food and aided conversation. It was a philosophy I had never encountered before but one which I was to embrace wholeheartedly during my stay. And I have to admit that as an educational tool it could not be bettered. These dinners never ended before ten o'clock so every day was rounded off for me with two hours relaxed (sometimes *very* relaxed) conversation in French. So the situation I found myself in was this: I either did my level best to join in and make some slight contribution to whatever was the topic of conversation for the day, or sit dumb and be thought an ignorant Englishman with no social graces. I tried to avoid the latter option.

In fact I did not have a great deal of choice in the matter. Monsieur was a retired teacher and was obviously relishing the opportunity of having a new pupil in his charge. Every night over dinner he would test me on my French verbs and encourage me to discuss politics, literature and God knows what else. There was a television in the corner of the sitting room but it played a very minor role in the day-to-day existence of the family. Apart from the news, it was only switched on if a film version of a classic from French literature was being shown or when General de Gaulle spoke to the nation about the situation in Algeria. But an absolute rule in the house was that the television was never on when a family meal was in progress . . . not even to hear what *le Général* had to say. Whatever it was it would keep.

My hosts were highly educated, cultured people who took learning and erudition very seriously. Messrs Dunn, Green and Forbes certainly knew what they were doing when they arranged this trip for me.

My room in the house was on the second floor and the view from the window ought to have been wonderful. Immediately in front of the house was a short garden edged by a dense hedge. Next was a road and then a row of trees which separated the inhabitants of the house from the River Seine. It should have been idyllic, but for the first week of my stay it certainly was not. This was Paris in the spring and so all the trees and flowers should have been in bloom, but they were not. It was just my luck to arrive during one of the coldest springs on record: there wasn't a daffodil in sight and the trees looked as naked and gaunt as they must have done the previous November. On the first night as I got ready to climb into bed I could feel an autumnal nip in the air and an unseasonal frost had been busy

View from the author's bedroom in Ablon-sur-Seine, Paris. *(Author's collection)*

designing weird and wonderful shapes on the window – an unexpected reminder of my arctic bedroom in Aintree.

But suddenly things changed, literally overnight. On about my fourth or fifth night chez Monsieur et Madame when I went to bed it was freezing but when I got up in the morning the sun was streaming through the window. Then, when I looked out of the window, I could not believe my eyes. Masses of deep green leaves had sprung as if from nowhere and smothered the whole line of trees in front of the house. When I opened the window a gust of heavily scented warm air seemed to rush past me and flood the room. Spring had arrived in all her glory and she looked beautiful. T.S. Eliot with his 'April is the cruellest month' must never have spent

The café-tabac in Ablon-sur-Seine, next-door to the restaurant Le Moulin Joyeux, which the author visited most days during his stay. *(Author's collection)*

Easter on the banks of the Seine! Or he must have known something about April that I didn't because his observation made no sense whatever from where I was standing.

In those days communications were nowhere near as sophisticated as they are today. Phoning England from France was still a complicated process with no guarantee of immediate success. And when you did eventually make a connection the cost was astronomical. So the thought of phoning home never even crossed my mind. Instead, as soon as I finished my breakfast on the first morning (a bowl of coffee, drunk like soup with a spoon, and the most delicious bread I had ever tasted, straight from the baker's and still warm), I set off to explore Ablon and find a postcard or two to send home. And the place to find postcards turned out to be a *café-tabac* where, at nine thirty in the morning I could sit down, write my postcards home and have a glass of beer. What a culture shock! Beer before my breakfast had even reached my stomach! Suddenly I found myself singing inwardly the lines of the popular song of the day, 'If they could see me now. . .'. I was going to mention the early morning tipple in my epistle home but then thought better of it. Dad would just say something like 'lucky so-and-so', but Mum would have told me to get on the next plane home. I knew exactly what would go through her mind: if I was drinking beer at that time in the morning, God knows what I'd be getting up to as the day wore on! As things turned out, however, I probably need not have been so paranoid. She had other worries which she had not mentioned to me before I left.

The first letter that arrived from home bore terrible news. It was from Dad telling me that Mum had been to the dentist who had informed her that she had a bad case of pyorrhoea and had then pulled out all her remaining front teeth: every one of them. So now she was waiting for a full set of dentures.

A couple of days later, when I had had time to get over the shock of her losing all her remaining teeth, I was in a bookshop in the centre of Paris which specialised in all things English: books, magazines, newspapers and greetings cards. One card caught my eye. On the front it had a drawing of Al Jolson, down on one knee and singing 'I'd walk a million miles for one of your smiles' and then on the inside in bold red letters it shouted at anyone who opened it: 'THE LEAST YOU COULD DO WAS PUT YOUR TEETH IN.' I thought of sending it but chickened out at the last minute. She might have been able to see the funny side of it, but on the other hand she might not.

Mr Dunn et al made sure I was not going to waste my time in Paris. They, no doubt, after coming to some private agreement with my mother, wanted me to benefit from the experience as much as possible, but they were also aware of the need to keep me busy. This was supposed to be an educational trip, not a holiday at the taxpayer's expense. So they enrolled me on a language course for foreigners at Paris's Sorbonne University for four or five hours a day classroom study. Pretty soon I settled down into a routine which was guaranteed to keep me out of mischief most of the time and yet allow me to get as much language practice as possible.

Every morning I would come down to the beautiful smell of fresh coffee (we only ever had tea at home), fresh bread and lovely creamy butter which Madame fetched from the market every morning before I was even out of bed. Then I would set off to the suburban train station and make my way into the centre of Paris for lessons. Back home in the evening I would have an hour or two doing my homework and then it was into the dining room again for another mammoth meal and stereophonic conversation which I had to try to keep up with. And that was the pattern for the rest of my stay.

But there was a more serious side to my visit, and one that friends and relatives back home in Aintree had understood. In the mid-1950s and early 1960s the Algerians were trying to break away from their colonial masters, the French. The French government wanted to retain power in Algeria and so a separatist war broke out between France and the FLN (the National Liberation Front). After a stalemate lasting a few years it looked as though the French government (under Mendès-France) was about to give in to the Algerians and this caused some renegade French officers to revolt and attempt to overturn the government, almost bringing the country to the verge of civil war in the process. General de Gaulle took control in June 1958, but the problem was not solved until Algeria finally gained independence in March 1962. So when I was there the situation was still very tense and the renegade French officers group, the OAS (*Organisation de l'Armée Secrète*), was still setting off the occasional terrorist bomb in Paris. And, judging by reports in the *News Chronicle* and the *Daily Express*, the threat of a full-scale civil war was still a distinct, if receding, possibility.

Occasionally, just occasionally, I stayed in the centre of Paris after classes and did not return to Ablon until nearly midnight. These were the few times when I decided I wanted to find out what all the fuss was about and see Paris at night. My first nocturnal stroll through the city was pleasant but uneventful. I called into a few bars to soak up some of the local colour and try my best at chatting to the natives.

But the second night was a bit more eventful than I would have wished. I had just come out of a café where I had enjoyed a few beers and a lively conversation with the barman about who suffered more in the war, la Grande Bretagne or la Belle France, when all of a sudden there was a flash, a loud bang and then the sound of tinkling glass. For a moment I and everyone else in the vicinity just stood in total silence and then all hell broke loose. People started screaming and running all over the place. Then within what seemed like minutes the fire engines arrived with their screaming sirens and, a short while after, ambulances started turning up as well.

As far as I know nobody was killed or even seriously injured. And I never found out what was the cause of the explosion. The papers the next day were not a lot of use as the event hardly received a mention. Those that did afford it some space merely speculated that it might have been a bomb, but the more probable explanation was a gas explosion or even that an oven in the café had, for some mysterious reason, exploded. I never did find out the real answer and would probably have forgotten all about it had it not been for a strange conversation I had with my mother when I returned home.

'Were you in any trouble when you were in Paris?' she suddenly said to me one day when we were on the bus going into town.

'Me? What kind of trouble? I wasn't in any trouble.' I hadn't told her about the 'bomb'.

'Are you sure?' she persisted. 'I was sitting in the front room putting my curlers in one night waiting for your Dad to come home. It was about ten or eleven o'clock and I heard you call "Mum! Mum!" It was like a loud whisper and I thought you'd come home early and were shouting through the letter box. That's the only way I can describe it.'

We were just passing the Astoria when she said this and it sent a shiver up my spine. The timing was almost exact: she must have heard my 'voice' in Aintree within seconds of the bomb (or gas main or oven) going off in Paris. How's that for extra-sensory perception?

The end of my time in Paris was not the happy event the rest of the stay might have led me to expect. Most evenings during the month or five weeks I was there we enjoyed convivial dinner conversations and discussions over Madame's superb cuisine. But I suddenly realised one day that our conversations covered just about every subject under the sun except one: the war. Most of the people I met in Paris were only too eager to talk about the war but it suddenly dawned upon me that for some reason the subject had never been broached in the Dupont household.

So on my last night there, just as Monsieur was pouring everyone a second glass of claret, I casually said something about the German occupation of France and you could have heard the proverbial pin drop.

'Ah,' said Monsieur, 'and tell me what you know of the occupation.'

So I did. Naively I started repeating everything I had been told about how dreadful life was 'under the Nazi jackboot' and how the Vichy government had betrayed France and those ideals of *liberté*, *égalité* and *fraternité* which gallant Frenchmen had fought and died for.

This was a mistake. It soon turned out that the whole family had actually supported Hitler and had got on very well with the German occupation forces. Monsieur even went on to say that Europe needed another Hitler to save us all from communism and/or the threat of Muslim domination. Giving in to the Arabs, as everybody expected de Gaulle to do, would be the beginning of the end.

I could not argue. My French had improved enormously while I had been in Paris, but Monsieur got so excited and carried away with his impassioned defence of the Germans that he forgot he was talking to a foreigner and rattled on faster and faster and totally failed to realise that I couldn't keep up with him. Eventually I had to excuse myself and say I needed an early night as I had an early train to catch the following morning. As I made my way upstairs I could hear Madame giving Monsieur a good old ticking off for speaking to me in such an impolite and aggressive manner.

The next morning it was Madame who saw me off, as Monsieur had already gone into Paris on 'urgent family business'. Perhaps he had, perhaps he had not. Was this a genuine reason or just an excuse? I don't know. All I can say is that I never saw either of them again.

25

A World of Difference

It was good to be home. I enjoyed the experience and adventure of Paris, but it was wonderful to savour the smells and sounds of Grace Road again. I arrived back at about seven o'clock one Saturday morning towards the end of April and, as I sat in the front room telling Dad what Paris was like, the smell of bacon and eggs drifted in from the kitchen where Mum was making the most delicious full English I ever tasted.

'What did you get for breakfast in France?' Mum asked as she plonked an enormous plate of bacon, eggs, fried bread, sausage and black pudding in front of me.

'A bowl of coffee and hot bread,' I replied.

'Is that all?' she retorted. 'Is that all the French have for breakfast? I think that's terrible.'

'But we normally only have a piece of toast and a cup of tea,' I said. 'When did we last have a fried breakfast like this one?'

'Well . . . yes . . . I suppose you're right.'

In a flash she had seen my side of the argument and agreed with me! What had happened while I had been away? I had never known Mum put up such a pathetic fight in an argument.

'Did the dentist extract your fighting spirit along with your teeth?' I ventured to joke with her. She roared with laughter. I could not believe it. I had never seen her like this. Normally a remark like that would have counted as insolence and merited a clip over the ear. But here she was being as nice as pie, not taking offence, not laying down the law and being (there's no other word for it) friendly.

Dad had a quiet word with me later. 'Don't worry, son,' he said. 'Your mother's just glad to have you back. She was worried about you, especially with all the trouble in Paris we keep hearing about. And apart from that, she's finally realised that you're not a child any more. You've grown up.'

He may have been right; I don't really know. I didn't feel particularly 'grown up' (what was that supposed to feel like?) but I probably had changed. Or, perhaps more accurately, my perception of the environment had changed. For some reason when I came back from Paris I had a different perspective on life, on Liverpool and Aintree. After spending over a month looking out of my bedroom window on to a line of beautiful trees and the River Seine, a certain period of adjustment was needed to get used to seeing nothing but the four-storey Territorial Army building (officially opened in the mid-1950s by a very young Shirley Bassey) which was the

The Territorial Army building opposite the house where the author grew up. Previously the building housed the offices of Vernons Pools. *(Liverpool Record Office)*

usual vista from my bedroom window in Grace Road. And Walton Vale, for so long the centre of my universe, lost some of its sparkle when I mentally compared it to the road by the Seine which I walked along every morning and evening as I made my way to and from the centre of Paris. And when I first travelled into Liverpool after my sojourn in France I have to confess that Lime Street, Church Street and Bold Street faded somewhat in comparison with the Champs-Elysées or la Place du Tertre in Montmartre. For some reason, when the waitress in the Kardomah asked in her inimitable Scouse accent 'Wha d'ya want, la'? Coffee?' the whole experience just seemed to lack some of the cachet that went with her Parisian counterpart's *'Café, Monsieur?'*

But it was not just my perception that was different. Changes were taking place in Liverpool, Aintree and doubtless everywhere else, but this was not a new phenomenon. The 1950s and '60s were both decades of change when social mores, habits and expectations took on altogether different characteristics and these changes, more often than not, were reflected in the environment. It was as if the authorities had decided that as they were clearing up the mess left after the war they might as well do a proper job and get rid of anything that would hamper the city's progress into the bright future everyone expected.

A shot of Walton Vale, early 1970s. The Radio Rentals shop had previously been Oddy's the greengrocers. *(Liverpool Record Office)*

One morning in the early fifties I was just emerging from a deep sleep and was still in that drowsy no-man's-land between dreams and reality but could already sense that something was wrong. I couldn't put my finger on it right away, but I just knew things were not as they should be. There was a strange sound coming from the direction of Walton Vale and it was slightly unnerving. I was still half asleep and could hear this odd noise . . . no I couldn't. When I opened my eyes I realised that what was so disturbing was not that I could hear a strange sound but that I couldn't hear a familiar one. A sound to which I had wakened up every morning since I had lived in that house was no longer to be heard. For the first time in my life I had opened my eyes in my bedroom in Grace Road and not heard the rattling of a tramcar. For the first time in almost a hundred years the good people of Aintree would have to travel to work by any means they could, but not by tram. It, like so much else at the time, was deemed to have outlived its usefulness and had been unceremoniously dumped on to history's sorry scrap-heap. More and more people were acquiring cars, petrol was cheap (about four shillings per gallon) and there simply was not enough room on the roads to cope with trams as well as all the new cars, buses, lorries and vans. So the tramcar had to go, and with it went one of the most memorable sounds of childhood for everyone born before 1957 when Liverpool's last remaining tram made its final journey.

But the removal of the trams from the main roads in Liverpool was not the swift, overnight operation it might seem. Yes, the actual vehicles did a miraculous vanishing act: one day they were running as normal past the end of Grace Road, the next day they weren't. But then began what seemed like the endless task of taking up all the tram-lines and removing the overhead cables which emanated from the centre of the city like a vast electrical cobweb. The terminus in Aintree was just by the Sefton Arms (at the entrance to the racecourse) and for weeks if not months the air vibrated with the noise of pneumatic drills as workmen spent their days digging up the old tram-lines, which had always seemed like a permanent feature of the scenery, all the way from the terminus to the very heart of the city. And the operation would have been going on all over Liverpool along all the other countless routes. It took most people quite a while to get used to Aintree without those dear old bone-shakers trundling along with their distinctive, ever-present rattling noise that provided an acoustic, almost orchestral, background accompaniment to all human activity in the area. As people worked, slept, ate, drank, listened to the radio, or stared up at the screen in the Walton Vale cinema they would always have been able to hear the muffled sound of the trams clunking along the road only a matter of a few yards away. And that clunking sound served as a comforting reminder that there was something unchanging in their lives.

Then one morning in the early fifties the good people of Aintree all had to face up to the fact that the trams would be heard no more and that nothing in the universe is permanent.

But the greatest change of all was ushered in with that other instrument of social engineering: television. When it arrived in the fifties it rang the death knell for the cinema culture as it had been known since its heyday way back in the twenties and thirties. Instead of queueing up outside a cinema on cold, wet winter evenings people found they could sit in the comfort of their own homes enjoying the new repast known as a 'TV supper' and refill their cups at will from a bottomless teapot.

Liverpool's last tram. The first one had clanked through Liverpool in March 1859. (*Catherine Rothwell*)

In the early days, when perhaps one neighbour in ten was affluent enough to be able to buy a telly, others would be invited round to view the new wonder and groups of friends would sit in the dark (presumably everyone thought that cinema conditions had to be recreated) and stare at the one-eyed god in the corner in total silence. Not for nothing did many express the opinion that television had destroyed the art of conversation.

Nor is it an exaggeration to point out the religious significance of the new invention. For many people the television set became an obsession if not an object of veneration and devotion as well as a status symbol. Possession of a television set was a distinct advantage to those who revelled in the never-ending struggle to keep ahead of the neighbours. Only a fridge could match it in the armoury of those who engaged in the constant battle of one-upmanship. All of a sudden the most urgent topic of conversation on the buses taking people into work every morning was the previous night's programmes on the box. Those who had televisions and could therefore contribute to the conversation felt somehow superior to those who still relied on the radio and the pictures for their evening entertainment. It became the 'must-have' of the generation picking itself up after the war, and it fitted in nicely with their aspirations of buying a semi-detached house with a little garden in the suburbs. And once acquired, the set would occupy pride of place in the owner's sitting room where it would be lovingly polished on an almost daily basis and not infrequently topped with a tastefully ornate vase of flowers. Some devotees would take things a stage further and cover the top of the television set with an embroidered cloth and so the whole ensemble came to resemble an altar. Then every evening, as soon as the evening meal was over, homage would commence to whichever deity was appearing on the nine- or twelve-inch screen that night. Cinema idols were replaced by sitting-room gods and goddesses and their 'congregations' sat in silent awe so as not to miss a single word from the surrogate pulpit.

One of the most devout families in Aintree must have been the Flynns. They were renowned for their Catholic devotion and made no secret of the fact that they went to Mass in the Blessed Sacrament Church every morning and three times on Sunday. Going into their house was like entering a church: crucifixes hung from every wall and door; there were pictures of 'Our Lord' or 'Our Lady' or the Pope or some saint in every room (even in the outside lav) so that a boy such as myself from a staunchly Protestant family felt somewhat intimidated (or frightened to death even) by all the religious paraphernalia. And if this was not enough, the most frightening thing of all was an almost life-size statue of Christ in the corner of the living room. As a five- or six-year-old I remember being scared stiff when I went into the room for the first time and saw this figure staring at me with cold grey eyes and pointing at me with his outstretched, rigid finger. But when the television was delivered, where did the Flynns put it? In the corner where the image of Christ had stood for donkeys' years. And what did they do with the Son of God? They carried him upstairs and deposited him in the loft where, for all I know, he might still be gathering dust today. The Flynns, like the rest of us, had been converted to the new religion.

Lennons supermarket on Warbreck Moor. The apex of the original Palace cinema roof can still be seen protruding above the new frontage. The building now houses an enormous shoe shop. *(Liverpool Record Office)*

The three cinemas within easy walking distance of Grace Road all suffered at the hands of television. The Walton Vale, where clients were greeted every evening by a very grand-looking commissionaire in full regalia (a crimson coat with gold-braid epaulettes) closed its doors for the last time in the early sixties, to be knocked down and rebuilt as a supermarket. The Palace on Warbreck Moor was transmogrified first of all into another supermarket (Lennons) and then into a vast, cavernous store selling cheap shoes. A little further away, over Orrell Park bridge and up Moss Lane, was the Carlton, which suffered the same fate as its nearer counterparts. It became a gathering place for the devotees of the other craze of the sixties, bingo.

Television's impact on the cinemas had a knock-on effect. TV closed down many cinemas (or 'picture-houses' as they were more generally known) at a time when another cultural revolution was taking place. The supermarket concept of shopping had been introduced from the United States and it spread like wild-fire through the whole country. In Aintree it meant that many of the small shopkeepers were put out of business simply because they could not compete with the new stores, which offered lower prices and greater convenience to the hard-pressed housewife trying to make ends meet. So television closed the cinemas and many of these were converted into supermarkets which in turn closed many of the smaller shops.

The Home and Colonial and Maypole were among the first to go. These had been wonderful food emporia where generations of Walton Vale families had shopped for groceries. In both places the shopkeepers wore slate-grey coats and offered customers a personal service that was totally absent from the newly arrived supermarkets. As they weighed out a pound of sugar and poured it into a brown paper bag for Mrs Dowling or cut a block of best butter and wrapped it in a piece of greaseproof paper for Mrs Fisher, they would chat and ask about their families and offer a smile if things were going well and a sympathetic ear when they weren't.

And then there were the wonderful smells. The sterile supermarkets with their pre-packet victuals couldn't hold a candle to the Home and Colonial or the May-pole, with their beguiling aromas of fresh food, spices and dried fruit. There was a romance about these shops which no supermarket could ever hope to match. One sniff as he or she entered the shop and the customer could be transported to far-away climes with palm-trees, dates, succulent exotic fruits and endless beaches gleaming white beneath a clear-blue sky. Unfortunately, romance lost out when shopping became purely functional, sterile and . . . cheaper!

So the idea of change should not have been all that strange to me when I came back from Paris. But it was. The very air seemed different, the smells seemed different and so did the light. I had been through a life-changing experience and was vaguely conscious of standing on the threshold of yet more changes. And I did not have to wait long for the first one.

A few nights after arriving home I went into the Windsor Castle for a drink with the lads. I was just finishing my first pint when I saw Dad standing a bit further down the bar. My first reaction was to shrink away and hope he hadn't seen me. But it was too late; he had spotted me, but his reaction was not at all what I expected. He just came up to me and, instead of telling me off or sending me home, he took a ten-shilling note out of his pocket and said 'What's your poison then, son?'

And that was that. I am not going to claim that I never went into a pub again, but something seemed to be missing from future visits. Dad bought me a pint, then I bought him one, and then we walked home and I went to bed. But I felt deflated. Much of the fun of going into a pub seemed to have vanished. Mum and Dad apparently knew all along that I had been frequenting the Windsor Castle and other similar watering holes. So that was probably my biggest personal change: I realised that the attraction of the pub was largely just the thought that I was getting away with doing something I should not have been doing.

Perhaps Dad was right; perhaps I had grown up.

26

Tending the Sick

My most immediate problem now was money. Staying on at school was fine on the one hand but it threw up some serious financial difficulties on the other. I passed my A levels in 1961 but decided to stay on for a third year in the sixth form to take what was then known as the scholarship exam. This was a wonderful year, as the basic idea of the exam was that the candidate should just read as widely as possible in his chosen subjects (mine were French and Spanish), write the odd essay and then take an exam at the end of the year. There were no set books to read and formal classroom lessons were kept to an absolute minimum. For most of the time I was left to my own devices and was expected to know how much work I needed to do.

But it did have its downside. For a start most of my friends in Aintree left school as soon as they could. They saw little point in staying on when there was a big world out there and plenty of opportunity to earn money. They could not understand why I would want to stay on, reading boring old books and writing useless essays when I could be enjoying the fruits of a job in a shipping office, working as a garage mechanic or unloading ships at the docks. They now always seemed to have plenty of money and could afford to go to the pub every night, buy second-hand cars to impress the girls with and even start thinking about going away on foreign holidays for a couple of weeks every summer. We were drifting apart psychologically as they could not understand my world and I could not understand theirs. A father of one friend summed up the chasm that was forming between us.

He had been an X-ray porter in Walton Hospital since the day he had been de-mobbed in 1945. This meant that for the last fifteen years or so he had walked along the same corridors taking patients to the X-ray department from their wards and then back to their wards from the X-ray department half an hour later. Day in, day out; every day the same. Never any change. From eight thirty in the morning until five in the evening for five days a week and then half a day on Saturdays, year in, year out. He never had to think for himself, make a decision or even talk to anybody if he did not want to. He just pushed the sick, the halt and the lame along endless corridors in a constant state of zomboid oblivion induced by the repetitive monotony of the job.

On one memorable night I got chatting to him in the Windsor Castle and he expressed a certain amusement at my wanting to stay on at school well beyond the age when people of his generation would have been only too glad to get out and start earning a living. Then he took his fag out of his mouth, coughed a bit and said,

The main entrance to Walton Hospital in the 1960s. *(Liverpool Record Office)*

'Wharra ya gonna be when ya leave college, den, Al?'

'I think I'll probably be a teacher,' I replied, although at that time I really did not know what I wanted to be.

'A teacher?' he spluttered. 'Bloody 'ell, wouldn't ya find dat borin'?'

How was I to answer that? I just sat speechless. If he thought teaching would be boring after spending God knows how long walking to and fro along the corridors of a converted Victorian workhouse I knew I would never be able to persuade him to the contrary.

And in a way it was just as well I said nothing. Had I opened my big mouth and entered into an argument with him about the benefits of education or the definition of monotony and boredom, the conversation would have soon developed into a dialogue of the deaf. His ideas of student life bore absolutely no resemblance to reality and my ideas of hospital portering were based solely on what he was telling me. I had no first-hand knowledge of working in a hospital and never expected to. But Fate had other plans which she was soon to reveal to me.

As I say, student penury was the bane of my life in the sixth form. I had no choice but to survive on the generosity of my parents, but they did not have all that much to splash around on themselves, to say nothing of supporting a son who many thought should have been out earning his own living by now. So in order to at least make some contribution to the family finances I took Saturday and holiday jobs as and when I could find them. One such job was on the WH Smith's bookstall on Central station; another involved selling ice-cream at the Liverpool Show one summer until I realised that my daily take-home pay was less than the bus fare to get to the venue. At Christmas I usually managed to get a job as a temporary postman helping out with the increased volume of mail. This could be quite rewarding financially as wages were usually supplemented by generous and grateful householders who honoured the age-old tradition of tipping even temporary postmen. And I remember a valuable lesson from those far-off days: the biggest tips were handed out by the people who inhabited some of the poorest areas of Liverpool. In the better-off districts tips could be minimal or, more often than not, non-existent.

But the best chance of contributing to the family finances came when I was offered casual employment as a porter in Walton Hospital. It was May or June 1962. I had finished school and was now at a loose end waiting to go to university in October and had a good few months when I could either go away on holiday at Mum and Dad's expense again or use the time to earn some cash. Guilt would not allow me to take any more off my parents and I was fed up never having two half-pennies to rub together so when I got the offer of earning about £7 for something like a fifty-hour working week at the hospital I grabbed the chance with both hands.

But I did make one request. The horror of X-ray portering with all the dreadful stories I had heard about doing the same thing day in, day out for weeks and months on end emboldened me to ask Mr Dunderdale, the head porter, if I could work just about anywhere else apart from the X-ray department. He laughed good-naturedly (I was later to grow to like his somewhat Falstaffian joviality) and assigned me to the general pool of porters so that I could be asked to go anywhere and do anything in almost any part of the hospital.

I had signed away my soul. I had agreed to do anything without fully understanding just what 'anything' could entail. Within hours of starting on the first morning I would have willingly traded the monotonous corridor-bashing for my first solo job. I was sitting in the porters' restroom when Mr Dunderdale came in carrying a bucket, mop and shovel. He handed me these implements of basic hygiene and asked if I knew where such-and-such a ward was. I foolishly admitted that I did know where the ward was and accepted the commission with a beginner's zeal. But I should have realised something was not quite right when I caught a glimpse of him winking at my fellow-porters.

I set off down the endless corridor, bucket in hand, on my way to the ward where, I had been informed, someone had spilled something that needed to be mopped up. It sounded like a perfectly ordinary run-of-the-mill sort of clearing-up job, and I suppose it would have been to a seasoned hospital porter. But to an absolute beginner like me it was the hospital equivalent of a baptism of fire.

As I got closer to the ward I gradually became aware of a strange smell. Walton Hospital, like all hospitals, was a veritable cauldron of smells of one kind or another. But there was something about this particular smell that was completely new to me. At first there was something sickeningly sweet about it but as I got closer and closer to the ward the 'sweet' got weaker and weaker and the 'sickening' got stronger and stronger. By the time I reached my destination the overpowering stench was making me feel sick. I could not imagine what could produce such a bad smell but as I turned the corner I found out. Some poor soul who had had his bowel removed had dropped his glass catheter bottle, which smashed and released its contents all over the floor. It seemed to me as if the whole corridor had been inundated with a foul-smelling, yellowy-brown liquid which was flowing gradually but inexorably in all directions. The ward sister, a rather plump, dark-haired Irish woman, snapped at me as if I was some kind of scum not much higher up the evolutionary scale than the malodorous mess I was expected to clean up, 'What are you gawping at? Don't just stand there. Get on with it. I'm just going down to the path lab and I'll be back in five minutes. I expect this lot to be cleaned up by the time I get back.'

By this time the smell was making me want to vomit. I could feel my guts tightening and an irrepressible retching sensation in my throat. I tried to fight it off and get on with the job, but it was too much for me. All of a sudden my hand shot up to my mouth in a desperate attempt to hold back the vomit which by now was coursing up my throat and into my mouth. The next thing I knew it had exploded through my fingers and shot through the air, stopping only when it came into contact with the front of a young doctor's crisp, beautifully ironed white coat as he came out of the staff toilets. He got such a shock seeing this technicolour vomit flying straight at him that he stepped back, slipped and fell right into the middle of the slimy, stinking gunge slithering about on the floor. Fortunately, and perhaps miraculously, he did not cut himself on the nasty shards of glass protruding from the disgusting sludge like polished diamonds glinting in the rays of the mid-morning sun.

Of course the patients in the ward could see all this through the open door at the end of the ward. It was the best entertainment some of them had had since D-Day and the man who laughed loudest was the old boy who had dropped the catheter bottle in the first place. Another who found it impossible to control his laughter burst the stitches holding his stomach together after an appendix operation a day or two earlier.

The only person for miles around who did not see the funny side (apart from the doctor and me) was the ward sister. She had expected to come back and find the corridor all spick and span as it had been before the unfortunate accident. Instead, the original mess had been compounded by my contribution of additional intestinal detritus and, worst of all, a young doctor had been humiliated and embarrassed by a lowly porter's inability to control his bodily reflexes. To say she was not pleased would be a perfect example of understatement.

In fact she was incandescent with rage. Never in the thirty years she had been a nurse had such a terrible thing happened to her. At least this is what she claimed, but, considering the sights I saw in the few months I worked in Walton Hospital, and with the benefit of hindsight, I think my little mishap was pretty far down on the scale of medical catastrophes. But at the time it seemed the most terrible thing that had ever happened to her and she threatened me in her lovely Irish brogue with fire and brimstone, hanging and the sack.

Fortunately Mr Dunderdale saved the day. He suddenly turned up with a couple of his porters, fully armed with all the accoutrements needed to clear up the mess. He had suspected that I might have failed on my first task and came along to inspect the damage. What confronted him was a little more than he expected but he took it with a good grace and told his battle-hardened foot soldiers to clean it all up. Then he turned his charm on the ward sister. Talk about soothing the savage beast! She melted as Mr Dunderdale smiled and explained that it was my first job on my first day and that no real harm was done. Her eyes gleamed as the head porter gave her a harmless cuddle and promised her he would be personally responsible for my actions in future.

'Oh, well,' she said in her lilting Galway accent, 'I suppose I can overlook it this once.' Then turning to me she added, obviously trying to cover up the tenderer side of her nature which had been exposed by Mr Dunderdale's irresistible charm, 'but don't let it happen again. I don't give second chances. Now away with you and be about your business.'

I did not need to be told a second time. I was off like a shot and hoped I would never have to return to the scene of that particular crime. But I was to return and very soon. In fact, less than an hour later I was back in the very same ward but this time the circumstances were very different.

I had been sent to do the first laundry round of the day. This entailed calling into a dozen or so wards and collecting bags of dirty or soiled linen and taking them down to the laundry. As I approached the scene of the unfortunate earlier occurrence I could hear a nurse speaking on the phone in the ward office.

'No . . . no . . . we're not sure . . . I think he's Italian but he might be Spanish or French . . . can you find someone who could interpret for us?'

I did not pay too much attention but my ears had pricked up at the mention of foreign languages. A minute or two later, as I was loading half a dozen brown paper laundry bags on to my trolley I overheard the follow-on conversation between the nurse and the ward sister from Galway. It was obvious from what they were saying that one of the patients was foreign and nobody could be sure what language he spoke, let alone communicate with him. He had been admitted with stomach pains but that was as much as anyone knew.

'Can I help?' I said, emboldened by the knowledge that the sister did have a softer side and that I just might be able to charm her the way Mr Dunderdale had done, particularly if I could help her in some way.

'What do you mean?' she said a little snootily.

'Well, I might at least be able to tell you what language he speaks.'

'Oh, all right,' she said incredulously. 'It's that man over there in the corner.'

I walked over to him and tried my French on him. He looked blank and shrugged his shoulders. Then I tried my Spanish and it worked like magic. He sat up in bed, smiled from ear to ear and shook me by the hand. He could communicate!

I spent the next half hour interpreting for the ward sister from Galway, who wanted to know who he was, how he came to be in Liverpool, where exactly his pains were, when they started and so on.

When she had all the information she wanted she took me into her little office, asked a nurse to make me a cup of tea and then wanted to know how I came to speak Spanish. I told her I was portering just for a few months before, I hoped, going off to university and her attitude immediately changed. I was no longer the unskilled skivvy she had previously taken me for. I was an educated member of the human race and as such deserved at least a modicum of respect. Never again did she tell me to clean up any revolting, stomach-turning messes or to 'be about my business'. In fact, whenever I saw her after that eventful day she always smiled and had a cheery word for me.

Ah, the benefits of a grammar-school education!

27

Pride & Prejudice

I had been working at the hospital for a few weeks when the letter arrived. I didn't have time to read it as I was late for work (if you were two minutes late clocking on you lost half an hour's pay), so I stuffed it in my pocket as I was running out of the house to catch the bus. Once settled on an upstairs seat I opened it and had to stifle the urge to jump up and shout the good news to the whole world. It was a personal letter from the Professor of Russian at Manchester University. He was impressed by my A level results and the fact that I had taught myself enough Russian to get a good pass at O level, and so was offering me a place on the degree course starting in October. I had done it. I was in.

When I got off the bus I ran all the way to the porters' restroom and, because of the extra boost of energy the good news had given me, actually clocked on with about five minutes to spare. But even if I had been late and lost half an hour's, an hour's or a whole day's pay I would not have cared. I was on a high or, as Dad used to say in such moments of extreme delight, I wouldn't have called the King my uncle. Now I had to tell Mum. She would still be on her way to work when I clocked on, so I had to wait until nine o'clock before I could slink off to the pay-phone by the main gates and convey the good news. I knew she would be as ecstatic as I was.

'Mum!' I shouted down into the receiver, 'I've done it! I'm in! I've got a letter from the professor . . . offering me a place!'

'Oh,' she said in muted tones. 'What professor? what subject?'

'Russian, of course. You knew I applied for Russian.'

'Well, I'm not happy about this,' she said trampling all over my enthusiasm and overflowing excitement. 'We'll have a talk about this when I get home tonight. Bye.' And she put the phone down.

All day I felt miserable. Before the phone call to Mum in her office I had been on cloud nine; all of a sudden I was down in the dumps. I thought she would have at least acknowledged my achievement, but she did not. We had been through all this nonsense a couple of years earlier and I thought I had convinced her that I knew what I wanted to study at university and that she had accepted it, albeit reluctantly. But now it seemed I was wrong. She still could not accept that fact that I wanted to study languages.

'Well, she'll just have to accept it,' I said to myself when I started to get over the feelings of dejection she had caused in me with her less than encouraging phone conversation.

'Tulloch!' yelled Mr Dunderdale, catching me walking back from the public telephone when I should have been doing the day's first laundry run. 'Did I just see you coming out of that telephone kiosk?'

'Yes, you did,' I replied with a mixture of guilt and anger in my voice. The problem was that porters were not supposed to make personal telephone calls during working hours and he would have been well within his rights to sack me on the spot. But he didn't. When I told him why I had disobeyed the rules and about Mum's reaction he did not exactly offer me a shoulder to cry on, but at least he could understand why I had done what I had done and why I was feeling so miserable.

'Never mind, lad,' he said, regaining some of the jovial tone which I normally associated with him. 'She'll come round, mothers always do. But until she does, there's work to be done here and I don't want to see you disappearing off to use the phone again.'

'OK,' I replied submissively and set off to make up for lost time collecting the dirty linen from the wards.

It was a beautiful summer's day and as the sun got higher and higher in the sky so the mercury in the thermometer seemed to shoot up as well. By early afternoon it was a scorcher.

I had just got back from my lunch-break and was asked to take the medical notes of somebody who had died in the morning over to the mortuary. In the early days of working at Walton Hospital trips to the mortuary (two or three times a week) filled me with trepidation, but by now I was well used to the sights that confronted me as I walked in through the door. Open coffins containing the mortal remains of the recently departed lying outside the autopsy room were at first a bit of a shock to the system, but I soon got used to them. I also got used to seeing autopsies themselves, as the big Polish pathologist and mortuary attendants were only too happy to explain the ins and outs of cutting up a dead body to anyone who was willing to listen.

So on this particular day I strolled over to the mortuary carrying the medical notes as per instructions. When I entered I noticed a couple of coffins lying just inside the door, one of which contained a depressingly young corpse. I strolled past them with my by now well-practised nonchalance and took the notes in to the office.

'Hello there, Al,' said Jim, one of the mortuary attendants, as I made my unannounced appearance. 'I'm just going to make a brew-up. Do you fancy a cuppa?'

'Don't mind if I do,' I replied as the heat was getting to me and a drink was just what I needed. 'Being kept busy?'

'No, it's dead quiet,' he said, and then burst out laughing at his own unconscious pun. 'Do you take milk and sugar?'

What happened next for some reason upset me more than seeing the dead bodies lined up outside the autopsy room. Jim stood up, strolled over to where the corpses were kept in refrigerated drawers and opened one. Inside, right next to a stiff, stood several bottles of milk.

'It's the only place I can keep the milk from going off in this hot weather,' he said, obviously noticing the look of surprise on my face.

Why should this upset me? After all, there was a practical logic at work here. The milk and the corpse both needed to be kept in cool conditions to prevent them from deteriorating. So why not keep them together in the same place? The only theory I could come up with at the time was that there was perhaps just a hint of disrespect associated with putting bottles of milk in a receptacle supposedly reserved for the dead. It was as if, subconsciously, I felt that the dead needed their space no less than the living and that we should respect their wishes. After all, none of us likes to have his or her personal space invaded when we are alive so why should we put up with it when we are dead?

I finished my tea and set off for the next task of the afternoon, the second laundry run. I was running a bit late and in danger of breaking one of the cardinal rules of hospital life: all laundry had to be collected from the wards before Matron's rounds.

Now in the strictly regimented hospital routine of those days the matron was roughly equivalent to a regimental sergeant major in the army. The surgeons and doctors were like the officer class, the ward sisters similar to sergeants and the nurses probably were the equivalent of the private soldiers. Everyone knew his or her position and role and it was part of the matron's brief to make sure nobody overstepped the mark or got ideas above his or her station. She also made sure we all did what was expected of us and in this way strict discipline was maintained. And her rounds were part of her technique for maintaining order and thus ensuring the cleanliness and efficiency of the whole hospital. They worked because they had two very simple purposes: on the one hand they allowed the matron to make sure that everybody was doing what he or she was supposed to be doing. If a medicine cupboard had been left unlocked or bedpans had not been thoroughly cleaned or there was dust under one of the beds, the matron would know whom to blame. On the other hand they allowed her to be seen. In the sixties matrons still wore the distinctive uniforms and dainty little bonnets we associate with Florence Nightingale, so there was absolutely no chance of her being mistaken for somebody else. Her uniform was a symbol of the authority she wielded and upon which the smooth running of the hospital depended.

Nor was there anything casual about her rounds. They were as rigorous as any barrack inspection and a porter or nurse who had not been doing his or her duty was in for a strict dressing down. The beginning of the ordeal would be announced by a sister or staff nurse coming through the door and announcing in as stentorian a voice as he or she could manage: 'Stand by your beds. Matron's round.'

Nurses would stand still at the end of the ward. It may have been different in female wards but ambulatory male patients had to stand smartly at the end of their beds. Those who were too ill to stand were allowed to stay in bed. What was definitely not allowed was for a patient to lie on his bed. The rule was 'Either in your bed or out of it, but definitely not on it.'

The round would then begin. Matron would walk slowly along each of the two rows of beds, examining the whole ward for neatness and cleanliness, making sure the beds had been properly made and that everything was ship-shape and Bristol fashion. She would occasionally stop and chat with one or two of the patients, asking them what they were in for and how they were being treated.

There were many rules in hospitals in those far-off days. It is no exaggeration to say that they were run like military institutions and such was the rigid hierarchy of authority that a patient in hospital for the first time might be forgiven for thinking he had fallen asleep and woken up in the army. Even friends and relatives visiting their loved ones in hospital were tolerated only if they agreed to abide by all the rules and regulations. Visiting hours were strictly controlled; perhaps half an hour in the morning and an hour at night, and visitors had to queue up outside the wards before the doors were opened by the ward sister on the dot of six. If Matron had not been satisfied by what she had seen during her round she would more often than not order the doors to remain closed until the fault had been put right. In the medical pantheon Matron may not have been God but she was not far below him.

Fortunately I was able to catch up on my duties and so avoided Matron's displeasure. It was one thing falling foul of the ward sister from Galway but the rough edge of Matron's tongue would have been a very different matter. Not even Mr Dunderdale's charm would have soothed her wrath, and the thought of him giving her even the most harmless of cuddles . . . no, it doesn't bear thinking about!

So I survived another day, almost. I had skirted the Scylla of Matron's fury but there still remained the little matter of negotiating the Charybdis of Mum's prejudice against all things cultural.

28

Bon Voyage!

When Mum came in she had a face like thunder. I had been miserable all day but she had obviously been in a state of repressed anger since she had put the phone down on me. For a while she said nothing, but just got on with making us all something to eat. She was in the kitchen and I was in the front room with Dad and Nan watching the six o'clock news. Then all of a sudden she opened the door and said, 'I want a word with you, come in the kitchen.'

It did flash across my mind that if Dad was right and she had realised that I had grown up this was not the message she was sending out. At this precise moment her tone of voice and choice of vocabulary were more reminiscent of the way she used to speak to me when she still thought of me as a child. But I said nothing. I was determined to save my powder for what was shaping up to be a lengthy battle.

'I thought I told you I didn't want you to waste your time at university studying languages.'

She did not hang about in an argument; she had a distinct preference for the full frontal attack with all guns blazing.

'We had this discussion last year,' I replied when I had recovered from the initial onslaught.

'Well, perhaps we did,' she said, 'but I thought that as you're working in a hospital now you might have given up those ideas and decided to work your way up to being a doctor.'

I could not believe my ears. Work my way up to being a doctor? Did she really think that was the way the system worked?

'You can't do that,' I answered. 'Porters stay porters all their working lives. If you want to be a doctor you have to go away to medical school and study and train for about six years.'

'Yes, I know that,' she said, 'but I thought you might have seen what it's like to be a doctor and changed your mind.'

'Look,' I said, feeling myself getting hot under the collar, 'I'm fed up with all these arguments about my future. I want to study Russian and that's all there is to it. If you want a doctor in the family, why don't you go off and be one?'

At this point Dad appeared. He had heard the row from the front room and was getting a little impatient. I thought he was on the brink of losing his temper for only the second time in my life. But his simmering ire was directed at Mum, not at me.

The author in his Manchester digs shortly after becoming a student at the university. *(Author's collection)*

'For goodness sake, can't you leave the lad alone?' he snapped at her. 'If he's not interested in medicine he's not interested in medicine. What have you got against him learning languages, anyway? For my money he's done well to get into university. Now can we just stop all these fights about what he's going to be? It's his life and he's quite capable of making his own mind up. What's for tea?'

And that was it. Mum never brought the subject up again. About six weeks later I was settled in digs in Manchester, an eager fresher about to embark on a privileged lifestyle of study and freedom. But before that I had to earn a bit more money and that meant I still had a few weeks work ahead of me at the hospital.

My initial fears of hospital portering being boring were never realised. It might have something to do with the fact that I spent only a couple of days working in the X-ray department, but my experience of working in Walton Hospital was one of constant change and variety. No two days were ever the same. And during the last few weeks I seemed to cram even more variety into each day than at any other time during the previous couple of months. Yes, the laundry run had to be done twice a day but I was not always involved with that. Some days I would have to help out in the kitchens, loading the hot food trolleys and then delivering them to the wards. Some days I would be assigned to the pathology laboratory and have to collect samples of various bodily fluids and excreta from the wards and bring them back for analysis. At one stage I found myself making a lot of trips to and from the 'Corridors of Power', the porters' affectionate term for the maternity ward. Some days I delivered the post to the wards and at other times I found myself working more as a filing clerk or temporary office worker relieving the regular staff who were away on holiday. I even did a stint in the Almoner's Office (now there's an expression from the past!), handling the older patients' old age pension arrangements while they were in hospital.

On my very last day I found myself back doing the laundry runs. I had just entered one of the last wards on my patch for the very last time and was putting the first of about half a dozen laundry bags on to the trolley when I heard what sounded like a fairly heated argument near one of the beds in the middle of the ward. I turned to see what was happening and just caught sight of a doctor making a cut-off gesture with his hands and saying to the Indian or Pakistani patient in the bed, 'I'm sorry, but that's all I have to say on the matter.'

And with that he turned away and walked off down the ward. As he was just about to open the door and disappear the gentleman in the bed yelled out at the top of his voice, in a beautiful Indian or Pakistani accent, 'May your face and rectum change places!'

I never found out what their disagreement had been about. It didn't matter. I and just about everybody else in the ward at the time roared with laughter. It was a wonderfully humorous note to finish on. As I walked down to the hospital gates for the last time I was still laughing. Even sitting on the bus home I couldn't suppress a private chuckle. I'm sure the other passengers thought I was mad.

The next morning I was free. I did not have to get up to catch the bus to work, and university was still some weeks away. I had saved up the magnificent sum of about £50 which in those days was at least a duke's if not exactly a king's ransom. Added to my term's grant of about £130 I was going to be able to live in comparative luxury until Christmas, when I was pretty confident I would be able to work as a temporary postman again for about four weeks. My immediate financial future was looking relatively rosy.

But freedom can have a strange feel to it. Aintree, where I was born and brought up and which was home for so long, all of a sudden seemed part of my past. My future was Manchester and my present felt like a kind of limbo hovering ethereally somewhere out along the East Lancs Road. And then, as summer faded and my preparations for my new life were nearly complete, I began to feel my excitement for the future mingle just slightly with a twinge of anticipatory homesickness. I also began to experience a certain lack of self-confidence and nurture embryonic doubts about university life. What if I failed my degree? What if I didn't even get as far as finals and failed at the first hurdle, the first-year exams? How would I feel if all the other students on my course were far cleverer than I was? Perhaps it would be better not to go there at all than fail and have to come back home and face the shame of defeat.

But these doubts did not last long. I soon convinced myself that if I'd got this far I would probably be able to cope. Then, one sunny Monday morning early in October 1962, my suitcases packed with clothes and a handful of textbooks and dictionaries, I got on the bus near the Walton Vale cinema (for the last time as a full-time Aintree resident) and headed into town. My immediate destination was Lime Street station and then I was off to Manchester. I was a student and wanted the whole world to know. I had already made up my mind that the first thing I would do when I arrived at the university would be to buy myself an Arts Faculty scarf.

Mum was a bit tearful and so was Nan as I walked across the threshold. Dad shook me by the hand, slipping a pound note into my jacket pocket as he did so. They all insisted that I phoned home that night to let them know I had found suitable digs and wasn't wandering the streets of Manchester like some down-and-out. It was a long farewell; the boy was leaving home and starting out on a long and perhaps hazardous journey. What perils would he meet on his way? How would he survive? Would there be fire-breathing dragons for him to contend with? Would he end up languishing in some dank and lonely dungeon guarded by hideous monsters? Would he always have a clean pair of underpants on and a clean handkerchief in his pocket? Manchester was like the other end of the known world.

I couldn't understand all the fuss. I had already decided that I was only going to be away during the week. I couldn't see the point of staying in Manchester at weekends where I knew nobody and, besides, I still wanted my Friday and Saturday nights out with the boys at the Cavern or in the Windsor Castle.

I was coming home on Friday.

Index